FINDING YOUR VOICE

COMMUNICATION SKILLS FOR CONFIDENT KIDS

DR. MINAKSHI BANSAL

DEDICATION

To my precious children, whose laughter, curiosity, and unwavering spirit inspired this book. May your voices always ring true, your words uplift others, and your hearts remain open to the boundless possibilities that emerge when we connect with one another.

ᐅᐅᐅ

Contents

Contents

Contents

Prayer

"Om Bhadram Karnebhih Shrinuyama Devah

Bhadram Pashyemakshabhiryajatrah

Sthirairangais Tushtuvamsastanubhih

Vyashema Devahitam Yadayuh

Svasti Na Indro Vriddhashravah

Svasti Nah Pusha Vishwavedah

Svasti Nastarkshyo Arishtanemih

Svasti No Brihaspatir Dadhatu

Om Shantih Shantih Shantih"

This mantra is a prayer for universal well-being, invoking the blessings of various deities for protection, health, and happiness. It emphasizes the importance of experiencing the auspicious through all senses and living a life aligned with divine purpose. The repetition of "Shantih" at the end signifies a deep desire for peace in the individual, the environment, and the universe at large. This mantra is often recited as a prayer for peace, prosperity, and the physical and spiritual well-being of all beings.

ॐॐॐ

About The Author

This book represents the culmination of extensive research and meticulous analysis, incorporating a diverse range of sources, including numerous books, scholarly studies, and personal experiences. Additionally, I have scoured various websites to gather relevant information and data essential for the compilation of this work. I have taken every precaution to ensure the accuracy of the information presented and have diligently cited all sources to acknowledge their contributions.

From her earliest days, Minakshi was distinguished by an insatiable appetite for reading. Her literary universe was inhabited by characters and narratives that spanned ethical tales, motivational and inspirational stories, and the mythic parables imbued with life lessons. This voracious reading habit was not merely for personal edification but was driven by a desire to distill and disseminate the essence of these narratives to foster the development of students and peers alike. She was particularly captivated by the lives and teachings of historical figures and spiritual leaders such as Adi Shankaracharya, Swami Vivekananda, Dr. APJ Abdul Kalam, Mahamana Pandit Madan Mohan Malviya, Mahatma Gandhi, Sardar Vallabhai Patel, and Vinoba Bhave, among others. Their philosophies and life stories fueled her ambition to embody their ideals of resilience, selflessness, and relentless pursuit of knowledge.

Dr. Minakshi's academic and practical engagement with psychology has been equally noteworthy. As a research scholar, her focus has been on exploring the intricate tapestry of the human psyche, aiming to unlock the potential for psychological well-being and societal harmony. Her scholarly work is complemented by her active involvement in social work, where she employs her academic insights to make tangible differences in the lives of the underprivileged. Her endeavours in social work are characterized by an innovative approach that combines traditional wisdom with contemporary psychological practices to address the multifaceted challenges faced by these communities.

Her artistic talents, another facet of her diverse capabilities, are not merely a personal passion but also serve as a medium through which she communicates and connects with others. Her art, rich in symbolism and emotional depth, reflects her philosophical inquiries and social concerns, offering viewers a glimpse into the breadth of her intellect and the depth of her compassion.

In addition to her contributions to the arts and social sciences, Dr. Minakshi has embraced the healing arts of Pranic Healing, mastering the techniques developed by Master Choa Kok Sui. This practice, which focuses on the manipulation of Prana or life energy to heal the body and aura, has been both a personal journey of discovery and a means through which she extends her healing touch to others. Her proficiency in Pranic Healing is complemented by her advocacy and teaching of various forms of meditation aimed at rejuvenation, personal betterment, and the cultivation of harmony within individuals and communities alike.

Dr. Minakshi's life is a narrative of relentless pursuit, not just of personal achievement but of the upliftment and empowerment of society at large. Her diverse interests and talents—spanning the arts, literature, psychology, and the healing practices—converge on a singular path of service. She embodies the spirit of the luminaries who inspired her, channelling their legacy through her actions and teachings. Through her books, art, and social initiatives, she continues to inspire a new generation to embark on their own journeys of self-discovery, resilience, and altruism.

Her commitment to social betterment, particularly her focus on uplifting underprivileged children, reflects a deep understanding of the transformative potential of education and personal development. By integrating her knowledge of psychology, her artistic sensibilities, and her healing practices, Dr. Bansal has developed a holistic approach to social work that addresses both the immediate needs and the long-term well-being of the communities she serves.

As an author, Dr. Minakshi's writings offer a blend of inspirational insights, practical wisdom, and reflective contemplations drawn from her extensive reading and life experiences. Her books serve as a guide for those seeking to navigate the complexities of life with grace, resilience, and purpose. Through her narratives, she extends an invitation to her readers to explore the depths of their own potential and to contribute meaningfully to the collective well-being of society.

In Dr. Minakshi Bansal, we find a remarkable synthesis of the artist, the scholar, the healer, and the social activist. Her life's work stands as a beacon of hope and a source of inspiration for individuals seeking to make a difference in the world. Her story is a compelling reminder of the power of individual action, rooted in compassion and driven by a profound commitment to the betterment of humanity. Dr. Minakshi's legacy is not just in the tangible outcomes of her efforts but in the enduring spirit of inquiry, empathy, and service that she embodies.

ᏡᏡᏡ

Preface

In a world brimming with digital connections and virtual interactions, the ability to communicate effectively in person remains an invaluable skill. For our young ones, navigating the complexities of social interactions, expressing their thoughts and feelings, and building lasting relationships are essential for their personal growth and future success.

As a mother, I have always been fascinated by the power of words and the profound impact they can have on our lives. From the tender lullabies whispered in the cradle to the animated conversations shared around the dinner table, words shape our perceptions, build our relationships, and ultimately, define who we are.

I believe that by equipping children with strong communication skills, we are giving them a gift that will last a lifetime, a gift that will open doors, forge connections, and enable them to make a positive impact on the world.

In this book, we embark on a journey of discovery, exploring the many facets of communication and its role in building confidence, empathy, and understanding. We delve into the nuances of verbal and nonverbal communication, the importance of active listening, the power of asking questions, and the art of expressing emotions in a healthy and constructive way.

Through engaging stories, practical tips, and fun activities, we guide children on a path towards becoming confident communicators who can express their thoughts and feelings with clarity and conviction.

We also recognize the importance of technology in today's world and offer guidance on how to navigate digital communication with respect, kindness, and integrity. We encourage children to embrace their unique voices, to use their words to uplift and inspire others, and to make a positive impact on their communities through effective communication.

This book is not just a guide for children; it is a resource for parents, teachers, and anyone who cares about empowering the next generation of communicators. By reading this book together, you can create a space for open dialogue, encourage children to practice their communication skills, and celebrate their successes along the way.

I am deeply grateful for the opportunity to share this book with you and your children. It is my hope that this book will inspire a lifelong love of learning, a passion for communication, and a commitment to using our voices to create a more connected and compassionate world.

As we embark on this journey together, I encourage you to approach each page with an open mind and a playful spirit. Let us embrace the power of words, the joy of connection, and the endless possibilities that emerge when we learn to communicate with confidence and compassion.

Dr. Minakshi Bansal
Social Activist
Ahmedabad, Gujarat, Bharat

ᐳᐳᐳ

ONE

HELLO, WORLD! INTRODUCING YOURSELF WITH A SMILE

In the grand tapestry of human connection, there exists a universal language that transcends cultural barriers and age differences: the language of a smile. From the moment we enter this world, we are greeted with smiles, and as we grow, we learn to reciprocate this simple yet powerful gesture. In the realm of communication, particularly for young learners, mastering the art of introducing oneself with a smile can set the stage for confident interactions and lasting friendships.

Imagine a scenario where a young child enters a room filled with unfamiliar faces. The air is thick with anticipation, and a sense of nervousness washes over them. However, with a deep breath and a conscious effort, a smile blossoms on their face, instantly transforming their demeanor. This smile acts as a beacon of warmth and approachability, inviting others to engage with them. It is a nonverbal signal that says, "I am friendly, open, and eager to connect."

The power of a smile lies in its ability to disarm and put others at ease. When we smile, we release endorphins, which are natural mood boosters that create a sense of happiness and well-being. This positive energy is contagious, and it radiates outwards, affecting those around us. A smiling face is like a magnet, drawing people in and making them feel comfortable and welcome.

For children, learning to introduce themselves with a smile is a fundamental building block for developing strong communication skills. It is a simple yet profound act that sets the tone for future interactions. When a child approaches a new person with a smile, they are not only expressing their own friendliness but also extending an invitation for connection. This initial gesture of goodwill can pave the way for meaningful conversations, shared experiences, and lasting bonds.

The impact of a smile goes beyond mere pleasantries. Research has shown that smiling can have a profound effect on our physical and mental health. When we smile, our brains release dopamine, a neurotransmitter associated with pleasure and reward. This chemical reaction not only makes us feel good but also strengthens our immune system and reduces stress levels. Smiling has also been linked to increased creativity, improved memory, and enhanced problem-solving skills.

In the context of communication, a smile can serve as a powerful tool for building rapport and establishing trust. When we smile at someone, we are signaling that we are non-threatening and approachable. This can be particularly important for children who are still developing their social skills and may feel hesitant or shy in new situations. A smile can help them overcome their initial anxieties and create a positive first impression.

Furthermore, a smile can enhance the effectiveness of verbal communication. When we speak with a smile, our words are infused with warmth and sincerity. Our tone of voice becomes more inviting, and our body language becomes more open and expressive. This combination of verbal and nonverbal cues creates a powerful message that is more likely to be received positively by others.

Teaching children the importance of introducing themselves with a smile is a valuable life skill that can benefit them in countless ways. It is a skill that can help them make friends, build relationships, and navigate social situations with confidence. By encouraging children to smile, we are empowering them to connect with others on a deeper level and create positive experiences that will last a lifetime.

In addition to the immediate benefits, introducing oneself with a smile can have long-term implications for a child's personal and professional development. When children learn to approach others with warmth and openness, they are more likely to be seen as approachable, likable, and trustworthy. These qualities can open doors to opportunities in both their personal and professional lives.

Moreover, a smile can be a powerful tool for diffusing conflict and resolving disagreements. When we smile at someone, we are signaling that we are willing to listen and understand their perspective. This can help de-escalate tense situations and create a more conducive environment for finding common ground.

In conclusion, the simple act of introducing oneself with a smile is a profound gesture that can have a transformative effect on our interactions with others. For children, learning to smile is a fundamental building block for developing strong communication skills, building relationships, and navigating social situations with confidence. By encouraging children to smile, we are empowering them to connect with others on a deeper level and create positive experiences that will last a lifetime. So, let us all embrace the power of a smile and use it to spread joy, warmth, and understanding throughout the world.

❥❥❥

A smile is your passport to new friendships. It speaks a language everyone understands, saying, "I'm friendly and ready to connect." So wear your smile proudly, and watch your world expand.

TWO
LOOK AT ME! MAKING EYE CONTACT SHOWS YOU CARE

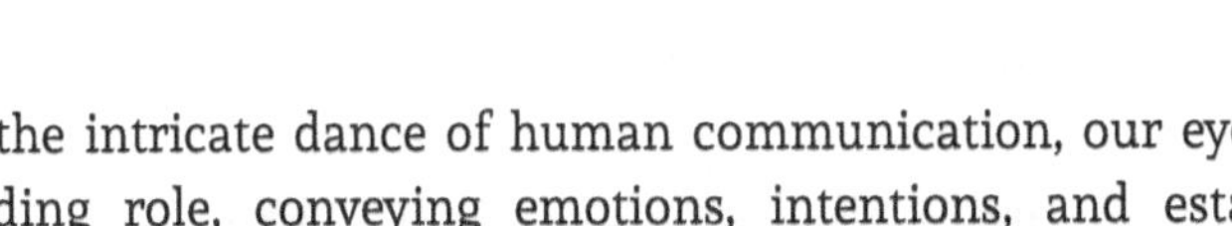

In the intricate dance of human communication, our eyes play a leading role, conveying emotions, intentions, and establishing connections that words alone cannot achieve. The simple act of making eye contact, especially for young learners, is a powerful tool that fosters understanding, trust, and empathy. It's a nonverbal signal that speaks volumes, conveying interest, respect, and a willingness to engage.

Imagine a child engaged in conversation with an adult. As the child speaks, their eyes dart around the room, avoiding direct contact. This lack of eye contact can create a sense of unease and disinterest, as if the child's attention is elsewhere. Now, imagine the same scenario, but with the child maintaining steady eye contact, their gaze fixed on the adult's face.

This simple shift transforms the dynamics of the interaction. The child appears more engaged, attentive, and invested in the conversation.

The power of eye contact lies in its ability to create a sense of intimacy and connection. When we look someone in the eyes, we are not only acknowledging their presence but also demonstrating our willingness to be fully present with them. This nonverbal cue communicates respect, attentiveness, and a genuine interest in what the other person has to say.

For children, learning to make eye contact is a crucial step in developing social and emotional intelligence. It is a skill that can help them build rapport with others, navigate social situations with confidence, and develop meaningful relationships. When children learn to look others in the eyes, they are not only communicating their own attentiveness but also fostering a sense of trust and understanding.

The impact of eye contact goes beyond mere social graces. Research has shown that making eye contact can trigger the release of oxytocin, a hormone associated with bonding and trust. This neurochemical reaction not only strengthens our connection with others but also reduces stress levels and promotes feelings of well-being. Eye contact has also been linked to increased empathy, improved communication, and enhanced persuasion.

In the context of communication, eye contact serves as a powerful tool for conveying sincerity and credibility. When we speak with someone and maintain eye contact, our words carry more weight and are perceived as more genuine. This can be particularly important for children who are still learning to express themselves verbally. By looking others in the eyes, they can reinforce their message and make a stronger impact.

Furthermore, eye contact can enhance the effectiveness of

nonverbal communication. Our eyes can convey a wide range of emotions, from joy and excitement to sadness and fear. By paying attention to the subtle cues in another person's eyes, we can gain valuable insights into their thoughts and feelings. This heightened awareness allows us to respond with empathy and understanding, further strengthening the bond between us.

Teaching children the importance of making eye contact is a valuable life skill that can benefit them in countless ways. It is a skill that can help them make friends, build relationships, and navigate social situations with confidence. By encouraging children to look others in the eyes, we are empowering them to connect with others on a deeper level and create positive experiences that will last a lifetime.

In addition to the immediate benefits, making eye contact can have long-term implications for a child's personal and professional development.

When children learn to engage with others through direct eye contact, they are more likely to be seen as confident, assertive, and trustworthy. These qualities can open doors to opportunities in both their personal and professional lives.

Moreover, eye contact can be a powerful tool for defusing conflict and resolving disagreements. When we look someone in the eyes, we are signaling that we are willing to listen and understand their perspective. This can help de-escalate tense situations and create a more conducive environment for finding common ground.

In conclusion, the simple act of making eye contact is a profound gesture that can have a transformative effect on our interactions with others. For children, learning to look others in the eyes is a crucial step in developing strong communication skills, building relationships, and navigating social situations with confidence.

By encouraging children to make eye contact, we are empowering them to connect with others on a deeper level and create positive experiences that will last a lifetime. So, let us all embrace the power of eye contact and use it to foster understanding, trust, and connection in our interactions with others.

ԲԲԲ

Your eyes are the windows to your soul. When you look someone in the eye, you're telling them, "I see you, I hear you, and I care." The connection you make can last a lifetime.

THREE

LISTEN UP! PAYING ATTENTION IS THE BEST WAY TO LEARN

In the symphony of human interaction, listening is not merely a passive act of hearing; it is an active engagement that unlocks the doors to understanding, learning, and growth. For young learners, cultivating the art of paying attention is not just a matter of good manners; it is the foundation upon which knowledge is built. It's a skill that empowers them to absorb information, make sense of the world around them, and develop critical thinking abilities.

Imagine a classroom bustling with activity. The teacher stands at the front, sharing fascinating stories and insightful explanations. However, some students are distracted, their minds wandering, their gaze fixed on anything but the teacher. These students miss out on valuable information, their learning stunted by their lack of attention. Now, picture the students who are fully present, their eyes locked on the teacher, their minds absorbing every word. These students are not only learning but also actively participating in the process, their understanding deepening with each passing moment.

The power of paying attention lies in its ability to focus our mental resources and create a receptive state for learning. When we listen attentively, we are not merely hearing sounds; we are actively processing information, making connections, and constructing meaning. This process of engagement strengthens our neural pathways, enhancing our cognitive abilities and paving the way for deeper understanding.

For children, learning to pay attention is a fundamental skill that underpins all aspects of their education. It is a skill that enables them to absorb information from various sources, whether it be a teacher's lecture, a book they are reading, or a conversation with a friend. When children learn to focus their attention, they are not only gaining knowledge but also developing critical thinking skills, such as analyzing information, evaluating evidence, and forming their own opinions.

The impact of paying attention extends beyond the classroom. In our increasingly information-saturated world, the ability to filter out distractions and focus on relevant information is more important than ever. Children who learn to pay attention are better equipped to navigate the complexities of modern life, make informed decisions, and achieve their goals.

Furthermore, paying attention is not just about acquiring knowledge; it is also about building relationships and fostering understanding. When we listen attentively to others, we are showing them respect and validating their experiences. This act of empathy strengthens our connection with them and creates a space for meaningful dialogue and collaboration.

Teaching children the importance of paying attention is a valuable life skill that can benefit them in countless ways. It is a skill that can help them succeed academically, build strong relationships, and make sound decisions. By encouraging children to listen attentively, we are empowering them to become active learners, critical thinkers, and compassionate individuals.

In addition to the immediate benefits, paying attention can have long-term implications for a child's personal and professional development. When children learn to focus their attention and engage with the world around them, they are more likely to be seen as intelligent, curious, and motivated. These qualities can open doors to opportunities in both their personal and professional lives.

Moreover, paying attention can be a powerful tool for personal growth and self-awareness. By listening attentively to our own thoughts and feelings, we can gain valuable insights into our motivations, values, and beliefs. This self-awareness can guide us in making decisions that are aligned with our authentic selves and lead to a more fulfilling life.

In conclusion, the art of paying attention is a profound practice that can unlock the doors to knowledge, understanding, and growth. For children, learning to focus their attention is a fundamental skill that underpins all aspects of their education and personal development. By encouraging children to listen attentively, we are empowering them to become active learners, critical thinkers, and compassionate individuals. So, let us all embrace the power of attention and use it to cultivate a deeper understanding of ourselves, our world, and each other.

ppp

Being a good listener is like having a superpower. You gain knowledge, build trust, and make others feel truly valued. Remember, the most meaningful conversations happen when we listen more than we speak.

FOUR

Ask Away! Curiosity Opens Doors

In the boundless landscape of human potential, curiosity stands as a beacon, illuminating the path to knowledge, understanding, and growth. For young learners, embracing the power of inquiry is not just a matter of asking questions; it is a mindset that propels them towards discovery, innovation, and a lifelong love of learning. It's a trait that transforms passive observers into active participants, eager to explore, experiment, and expand their horizons.

Imagine a child standing before a vast and intricate machine, their eyes wide with wonder. They reach out to touch its gleaming surface, their fingers tracing its contours. "How does it work?" they ask, their voice filled with genuine curiosity. This simple question sparks a chain reaction, igniting a desire to understand, to delve deeper, to uncover the hidden mechanisms that make the machine tick. It is a moment of pure inquisitiveness, unburdened by fear or self-doubt.

The power of asking questions lies in its ability to open doors that would otherwise remain closed. When we ask questions, we are not merely seeking information; we are actively engaging with the world around us, challenging assumptions, and seeking new perspectives. This process of inquiry fuels our intellectual growth, expands our knowledge base, and cultivates a spirit of lifelong learning.

For children, curiosity is an innate gift, a natural instinct that drives them to explore, experiment, and make sense of the world around them. It is a force that propels them to ask "why" and "how" incessantly, to seek answers to their burning questions, and to unravel the mysteries that lie hidden in plain sight. When children are encouraged to ask questions, they are not only satisfying their own curiosity but also developing critical thinking skills, such as problem-solving, analysis, and evaluation.

The impact of asking questions extends beyond the realm of personal development. In our ever-evolving society, the ability to ask insightful questions is a valuable asset. It is a skill that enables us to challenge the status quo, identify opportunities for innovation, and drive meaningful change. Children who are encouraged to ask questions are more likely to become independent thinkers, creative problem solvers, and active contributors to society.

Furthermore, asking questions is not just about seeking information; it is also about building relationships and fostering collaboration. When we ask questions, we are demonstrating our interest in others and inviting them to share their knowledge and experiences. This act of reciprocity strengthens our connection with them and creates a space for mutual learning and growth.

Teaching children the importance of asking questions is a valuable life skill that can benefit them in countless ways. It is a skill that can help them succeed academically, thrive professionally, and make informed decisions throughout their lives. By encouraging children to ask questions, we are empowering them to become active learners, critical thinkers, and engaged citizens.

In addition to the immediate benefits, asking questions can have a profound impact on a child's long-term development. When children are encouraged to question the world around them, they are more likely to develop a strong sense of self-efficacy, believing in their ability to learn and grow. This self-belief can fuel their motivation, resilience, and ultimately, their success.

Moreover, asking questions can be a powerful tool for personal transformation. By questioning our own assumptions and beliefs, we can challenge our biases, expand our perspectives, and open ourselves up to new possibilities. This process of self-reflection can lead to greater self-awareness, personal growth, and a more fulfilling life.

In conclusion, the act of asking questions is a gateway to a world of possibilities. It is a force that drives us to explore, discover, and create. For children, curiosity is a precious gift, a natural instinct that should be nurtured and encouraged. By fostering a culture of inquiry, we are empowering children to become active learners, critical thinkers, and compassionate individuals. So, let us all embrace the power of asking questions and use it to unlock our full potential, both individually and collectively. Ask away, for curiosity is the key that opens doors to a brighter future.

Don't be afraid to ask questions! Curiosity is the key to unlocking a world of knowledge and understanding. The more you ask, the more you'll learn and the more you'll grow.

FIVE

WORDS MATTER! CHOOSING KIND WORDS MAKES EVERYONE FEEL GOOD

In the intricate tapestry of human interaction, words wield immense power. They have the ability to uplift or tear down, to heal or wound, to connect or isolate. For young learners, understanding the profound impact of words is a crucial step in developing empathy, compassion, and healthy relationships. The conscious choice to use kind words is not merely a matter of politeness; it is a transformative act that ripples outwards, creating a positive and nurturing environment for everyone involved.

Imagine a playground filled with children engaged in various activities. In one corner, a group of children is laughing and playing together, their words filled with encouragement and support. In another corner, a lone child sits apart, their head bowed, their ears ringing with the harsh words of a bully. These two scenarios paint a stark contrast, highlighting the profound impact that words can have on our emotional well-being and social interactions.

The power of kind words lies in their ability to create a sense of safety, belonging, and connection. When we use kind words, we are not only expressing our own positive intentions but also affirming the inherent worth and dignity of others. This act of validation can have a profound effect on a person's self-esteem, confidence, and overall sense of well-being.

For children, learning to use kind words is a fundamental building block for developing healthy relationships. It is a skill that teaches them to consider the feelings of others, to communicate with empathy and respect, and to build bridges of understanding. When children use kind words, they are not only making others feel good but also creating a positive feedback loop that reinforces their own positive behaviors.

The impact of kind words extends beyond the immediate context of an interaction. Research has shown that the use of kind words can have a ripple effect, spreading positivity and goodwill throughout a community. When we choose to speak kindly to others, we are not only making them feel good but also inspiring them to act kindly towards others. This chain reaction of kindness can create a more compassionate and supportive environment for everyone.

Furthermore, the use of kind words is not just about being nice; it is also about effective communication. When we speak with kindness, our words are more likely to be heard and understood. People are more receptive to our message when it is delivered with warmth and sincerity. This can be particularly important for children who are still developing their communication skills. By using kind words, they can create a more positive and productive dialogue with others.

Teaching children the importance of using kind words is a valuable life skill that can benefit them in countless ways. It is a skill that can help them make friends, build relationships, resolve conflicts peacefully, and navigate social situations with grace and confidence. By encouraging children to use kind words, we are empowering them to become compassionate leaders, effective communicators, and positive contributors to society.

In addition to the immediate benefits, the use of kind words can have long-term implications for a child's personal and professional development. When children learn to communicate with kindness, they are more likely to be seen as trustworthy, approachable, and cooperative. These qualities can open doors to opportunities in both their personal and professional lives.

Moreover, the use of kind words can be a powerful tool for personal growth and self-awareness. When we speak kindly to others, we are also reinforcing positive self-talk and cultivating a more compassionate and understanding relationship with ourselves. This inner kindness can lead to greater self-acceptance, self-love, and overall well-being.

In conclusion, the words we choose matter. They have the power to shape our relationships, our communities, and our world. For children, learning to use kind words is a fundamental skill that lays the foundation for a lifetime of positive interactions and meaningful connections. By encouraging children to speak with kindness, we are empowering them to become compassionate leaders, effective communicators, and agents of positive change. So, let us all embrace the power of kind words and use them to create a more loving, supportive, and harmonious world for ourselves and for generations to come.

ppp

Your words have the power to build bridges or create barriers. Choose kind words that uplift and inspire others. Remember, a single compliment can brighten someone's day and create a ripple effect of positivity.

SIX

Speak Clearly! Use Your Voice So Everyone Can Understand

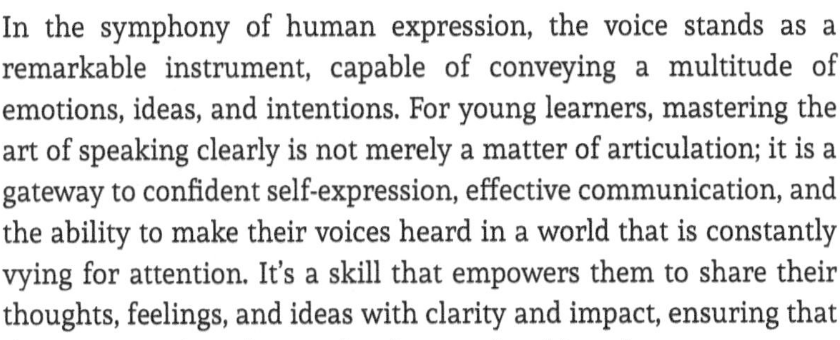

In the symphony of human expression, the voice stands as a remarkable instrument, capable of conveying a multitude of emotions, ideas, and intentions. For young learners, mastering the art of speaking clearly is not merely a matter of articulation; it is a gateway to confident self-expression, effective communication, and the ability to make their voices heard in a world that is constantly vying for attention. It's a skill that empowers them to share their thoughts, feelings, and ideas with clarity and impact, ensuring that their message is understood and appreciated by others.

Imagine a child standing on a stage, their voice trembling as they deliver a speech. Their words are mumbled, their sentences fragmented, and their message lost in a sea of uncertainty. Now, picture the same child, their voice strong and clear, their words flowing effortlessly, their message resonating with the audience. This transformation highlights the profound impact that clear speech can have on our ability to connect with others and make a lasting impression.

The power of speaking clearly lies in its ability to create a bridge of understanding between individuals. When we articulate our thoughts and feelings with clarity and precision, we are not only conveying information but also inviting others to share in our experiences and perspectives. This shared understanding fosters empathy, builds trust, and strengthens relationships.

For children, learning to speak clearly is a fundamental skill that underpins all aspects of their communication. It is a skill that enables them to express their needs and desires, share their ideas and opinions, and participate in meaningful conversations. When children speak clearly, they are not only communicating effectively but also building confidence in their own voices and asserting their presence in the world.

The impact of clear speech extends beyond interpersonal interactions. In academic settings, the ability to articulate one's thoughts clearly is essential for success. Whether it's answering questions in class, participating in discussions, or delivering presentations, clear speech allows children to showcase their knowledge and understanding, earning the respect of their teachers and peers.

Furthermore, clear speech is a valuable asset in the professional world. Effective communication is a key ingredient for success in any career, and the ability to speak clearly and confidently is highly valued by employers. Children who learn to articulate their thoughts and ideas clearly are more likely to excel in job interviews, presentations, and team collaborations.

The benefits of speaking clearly are not limited to external achievements. On a personal level, clear speech can empower individuals to express their authentic selves and advocate for their needs and desires. When we speak clearly, we are more likely to be heard and taken seriously. This can lead to greater self-confidence, self-esteem, and overall well-being.

Teaching children the importance of speaking clearly is a valuable investment in their future. It is a skill that can be nurtured and developed through practice, feedback, and encouragement. By providing children with opportunities to express themselves verbally in a safe and supportive environment, we can help them overcome their inhibitions, refine their communication skills, and discover the power of their own voices.

In addition to the immediate benefits, clear speech can have long-term implications for a child's personal and professional development. When children learn to communicate effectively, they are more likely to be seen as confident, articulate, and persuasive. These qualities can open doors to opportunities in both their personal and professional lives.

Moreover, clear speech can be a powerful tool for social change. When we speak clearly and passionately about the issues that matter to us, we can inspire others to take action and create a more just and equitable world. Children who learn to use their voices for good can become agents of change, advocating for their communities and making a positive impact on the world.

In conclusion, the act of speaking clearly is a gift that we can give ourselves and others. It is a skill that empowers us to connect with others, share our ideas, and make a difference in the world. For children, learning to speak clearly is a fundamental building block for a lifetime of effective communication, personal growth, and social impact. By nurturing this skill in our children, we are not only giving them the tools to succeed but also empowering them to become confident, articulate, and compassionate individuals who can make their voices heard and their presence felt in the world. So, let us all speak clearly, for our words have the power to inspire, inform, and transform.

ϸϸϸ

Speak your truth with confidence and clarity. Your voice matters, and the world deserves to hear what you have to say. Remember, the most powerful voices are those that speak from the heart.

SEVEN

I Feel... Sharing Your Feelings Helps Others Understand You

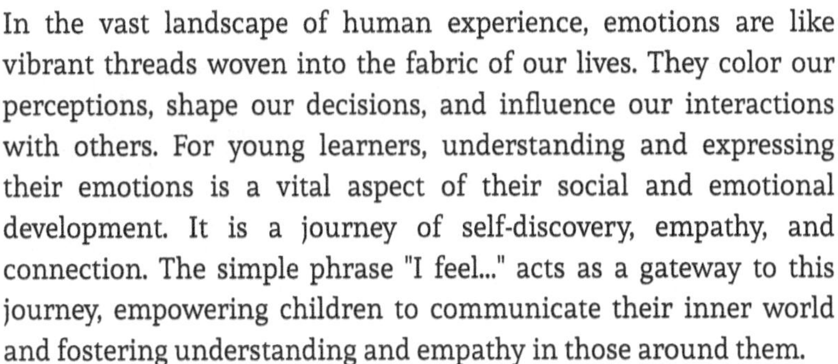

In the vast landscape of human experience, emotions are like vibrant threads woven into the fabric of our lives. They color our perceptions, shape our decisions, and influence our interactions with others. For young learners, understanding and expressing their emotions is a vital aspect of their social and emotional development. It is a journey of self-discovery, empathy, and connection. The simple phrase "I feel..." acts as a gateway to this journey, empowering children to communicate their inner world and fostering understanding and empathy in those around them.

Imagine a child sitting alone on a swing, their face etched with sadness. Their heart feels heavy, their thoughts clouded with worry. They long to share their feelings, but the words seem stuck in their throat. With a gentle nudge from a caring adult, they muster the courage to utter those two simple words: "I feel..." In that moment, a floodgate opens, releasing a torrent of emotions that have been bottled up inside. The child begins to describe their sadness, their worries, their fears. As they speak, their burden lightens, their heart begins to heal.

The power of expressing emotions lies in its ability to bridge the gap between our inner world and the outer world. When we share our feelings, we are not only giving voice to our own experiences but also inviting others to share in our emotional landscape. This act of vulnerability creates a space for empathy, understanding, and connection.

For children, learning to express their emotions is a fundamental skill that underpins their social and emotional development. It is a skill that enables them to communicate their needs and desires, navigate complex social situations, and build healthy relationships. When children learn to say "I feel...", they are not only expressing themselves but also developing emotional intelligence, self-awareness, and empathy.

The impact of expressing emotions extends beyond personal well-being. Research has shown that emotional expression can have a profound effect on our physical and mental health. When we suppress our emotions, we are essentially bottling up stress, which can lead to a host of physical and mental ailments. Conversely, when we express our emotions in a healthy way, we are releasing this pent-up stress, promoting emotional regulation, and fostering a sense of well-being.

In the context of communication, expressing emotions is a powerful tool for building rapport and establishing trust. When we share our feelings with others, we are signaling that we are open, honest, and vulnerable. This vulnerability can be disarming, encouraging others to reciprocate with their own openness and honesty. This mutual exchange of emotions creates a deeper level of connection and understanding.

Furthermore, expressing emotions is not just about venting or seeking validation; it is also about problem-solving and conflict resolution. When we are able to articulate our feelings clearly and calmly, we are better equipped to address the root causes of our conflicts and find mutually agreeable solutions. This is particularly important for children who are still learning to navigate the complexities of social interactions.

Teaching children the importance of expressing their emotions is a gift that will last a lifetime. It is a skill that will empower them to build strong relationships, navigate challenging situations, and lead fulfilling lives. By creating a safe and supportive environment where children feel comfortable expressing their feelings, we are nurturing their emotional intelligence and setting them on a path towards a happier and healthier future.

In addition to the immediate benefits, expressing emotions can have long-term implications for a child's personal and professional development. When children learn to communicate their emotions effectively, they are more likely to be seen as self-aware, empathetic, and emotionally intelligent. These qualities are highly valued in both personal and professional relationships and can open doors to opportunities in all areas of life.

Moreover, expressing emotions can be a powerful tool for social change. When we speak out about the injustices we witness or the pain we experience, we are raising awareness and inspiring others to take action. Children who learn to use their voices to express their emotions can become powerful advocates for themselves and others, creating a more compassionate and equitable world.

In conclusion, the phrase "I feel..." is more than just a statement; it is an invitation to connect, to understand, and to empathize. For children, learning to express their emotions is a transformative journey that can lead to greater self-awareness, healthier relationships, and a more fulfilling life. By encouraging children to share their feelings, we are not only empowering them to be their authentic selves but also fostering a more compassionate and understanding society. So, let us all embrace the power of emotions and use it to build bridges, heal wounds, and create a world where everyone feels seen, heard, and valued.

♥♥♥

Your feelings are valid, and expressing them is a sign of strength, not weakness. Sharing your emotions opens the door to understanding, empathy, and deeper connections with others.

EIGHT

TELL ME MORE! ASKING QUESTIONS SHOWS YOU'RE INTERESTED

In the vast landscape of human communication, questions serve as a vital tool for exploration, understanding, and connection. For young learners, embracing the art of asking questions is not merely a matter of seeking information; it is a mindset that fosters curiosity, critical thinking, and a lifelong thirst for knowledge. It's a skill that transforms passive observers into active participants, eager to delve deeper, challenge assumptions, and expand their understanding of the world around them.

Imagine a child standing before a majestic oak tree, its branches reaching towards the sky. They gaze up in awe, marveling at its size and strength. "How old is this tree?" they ask, their voice filled with wonder. This simple question sparks a chain reaction, igniting a desire to learn more about the tree's history, its life cycle, and its role in the ecosystem. It is a moment of pure curiosity, unburdened by fear or self-doubt.

The power of asking questions lies in its ability to open doors that would otherwise remain closed. When we ask questions, we are not merely seeking answers; we are actively engaging with the world around us, challenging our assumptions, and seeking new perspectives. This process of inquiry fuels our intellectual growth, expands our knowledge base, and cultivates a spirit of lifelong learning.

For children, asking questions is an innate drive, a natural instinct that propels them to explore, experiment, and make sense of the world around them. It is a force that drives them to ask "why" and "how" incessantly, to seek answers to their burning questions, and to unravel the mysteries that lie hidden in plain sight. When children are encouraged to ask questions, they are not only satisfying their own curiosity but also developing critical thinking skills, such as problem-solving, analysis, and evaluation.

The impact of asking questions extends beyond the realm of personal development. In our ever-evolving society, the ability to ask insightful questions is a valuable asset. It is a skill that enables us to challenge the status quo, identify opportunities for innovation, and drive meaningful change. Children who are encouraged to ask questions are more likely to become independent thinkers, creative problem solvers, and active contributors to society.

Furthermore, asking questions is not just about seeking information; it is also about building relationships and fostering collaboration. When we ask questions, we are demonstrating our interest in others and inviting them to share their knowledge and experiences. This act of reciprocity strengthens our connection with them and creates a space for mutual learning and growth.

In the context of communication, asking questions is a powerful tool for building rapport and establishing trust. When we ask questions, we are signaling that we are listening, that we value the other person's perspective, and that we are genuinely interested in what they have to say. This can be particularly important for children who are still developing their social skills and may feel hesitant or shy in new situations. Asking questions can help them break the ice, initiate conversations, and build meaningful connections with others.

Moreover, asking questions can be a catalyst for creativity and innovation. When we challenge ourselves to think outside the box and question the conventional wisdom, we open ourselves up to new possibilities and solutions. This is why asking questions is at the heart of scientific inquiry, artistic expression, and entrepreneurial endeavors.

Teaching children the importance of asking questions is a valuable investment in their future. It is a skill that can be nurtured and developed through practice, encouragement, and a willingness to embrace the unknown. By creating a safe and supportive environment where children feel comfortable asking questions, we are empowering them to become curious, engaged, and lifelong learners.

In addition to the immediate benefits, asking questions can have a profound impact on a child's long-term development. When children are encouraged to question the world around them, they are more likely to develop a strong sense of self-efficacy, believing in their ability to learn and grow. This self-belief can fuel their motivation, resilience, and ultimately, their success.

Furthermore, asking questions can be a powerful tool for personal transformation. By questioning our own assumptions and beliefs, we can challenge our biases, expand our perspectives, and open ourselves up to new possibilities. This process of self-reflection can lead to greater self-awareness, personal growth, and a more fulfilling life.

In conclusion, the act of asking questions is a gateway to a world of knowledge, understanding, and connection. For children, curiosity is a precious gift, a natural instinct that should be nurtured and encouraged. By fostering a culture of inquiry, we are empowering children to become active learners, critical thinkers, and compassionate individuals. So, let us all embrace the power of asking questions and use it to unlock our full potential, both individually and collectively. Tell me more, for questions are the keys that unlock the doors to a brighter future.

ᐅᐅᐅ

Don't be afraid to ask, "Tell me more." It shows you're engaged, curious, and eager to learn. The more you ask, the more you'll discover about the world and the people around you.

NINE

TAKE TURNS! GOOD CONVERSATIONS MEAN EVERYONE GETS A CHANCE TO TALK

In the intricate ballet of human interaction, conversation is a dynamic and collaborative performance, where each participant plays a vital role. Like dancers gracefully alternating between leading and following, effective communicators understand the importance of taking turns. For young learners, mastering this fundamental skill is not just a matter of etiquette; it is a gateway to deeper understanding, stronger connections, and a richer exchange of ideas. It's a practice that fosters respect, empathy, and a sense of shared purpose, transforming simple exchanges into meaningful dialogues that leave a lasting impact.

Imagine a group of children gathered around a campfire, sharing stories and experiences. As one child speaks, the others listen attentively, their faces alight with interest and curiosity. When the story concludes, another child picks up the thread, seamlessly weaving their own narrative into the tapestry of the conversation. This harmonious exchange of stories creates a sense of unity and belonging, as each child's voice is heard and valued.

The power of taking turns lies in its ability to create a balanced and equitable space for communication. When we take turns speaking and listening, we are not only showing respect for others but also creating an environment where everyone feels heard and valued. This shared experience fosters a sense of community and belonging, as each participant contributes to the collective wisdom and understanding of the group.

For children, learning to take turns is a crucial step in developing social and emotional intelligence. It is a skill that teaches them to be mindful of others, to listen attentively, and to wait patiently for their turn to speak. When children learn to take turns, they are not only developing their communication skills but also cultivating empathy, patience, and a sense of fairness.

The impact of taking turns extends beyond interpersonal interactions. In academic settings, the ability to take turns speaking and listening is essential for effective collaboration and knowledge sharing. Whether it's working on group projects, participating in class discussions, or engaging in debates, taking turns allows students to learn from each other, challenge each other's perspectives, and arrive at more nuanced and informed conclusions.

Furthermore, taking turns is a valuable asset in the professional world. Effective communication is a key ingredient for success in any career, and the ability to listen actively and respond thoughtfully is highly valued by employers. Children who learn to take turns speaking and listening are more likely to excel in team collaborations, negotiations, and client interactions.

The benefits of taking turns are not limited to external achievements. On a personal level, taking turns can enrich our relationships and deepen our connections with others. When we actively listen to others and give them the space to express themselves, we are showing them that we care about their thoughts and feelings. This act of validation can strengthen our bonds with others and foster a sense of mutual respect and understanding.

Teaching children the importance of taking turns is a gift that will last a lifetime. It is a skill that will empower them to build strong relationships, navigate social situations with grace, and participate in meaningful dialogues. By modeling turn-taking behavior and creating opportunities for children to practice this skill, we can help them develop the communication skills necessary for success in all areas of life.

In addition to the immediate benefits, taking turns can have long-term implications for a child's personal and professional development. When children learn to listen attentively and respond thoughtfully to others, they are more likely to be seen as respectful, collaborative, and emotionally intelligent. These qualities can open doors to opportunities in both their personal and professional lives.

Moreover, taking turns can be a powerful tool for social change. When we create spaces where everyone's voice is heard and valued, we are fostering a more inclusive and equitable society. Children who learn to take turns speaking and listening are more likely to become engaged citizens who actively participate in civic discourse and work towards a better future for all.

In conclusion, the act of taking turns is a dance of conversation, a harmonious exchange of ideas and perspectives that enriches our lives and strengthens our connections with others. For children, learning to take turns is a fundamental skill that lays the foundation for effective communication, healthy relationships, and a lifelong love of learning. By fostering a culture of respect and turn-taking, we are empowering children to become empathetic listeners, thoughtful speakers, and active participants in the world around them. So, let us all embrace the rhythm of conversation, taking turns to share our voices, listen to others, and create a symphony of understanding that resonates throughout our lives.

ppp

Conversation is a dance, not a monologue. Take turns sharing your thoughts and listening to others. Remember, the best conversations are those where everyone feels heard and valued.

TEN

BODY TALK! YOUR BODY LANGUAGE SAYS A LOT

In the intricate dance of human interaction, our bodies are constantly communicating, often revealing more than our words ever could. From the subtle tilt of a head to the expansive gesture of open arms, our nonverbal cues speak volumes about our thoughts, feelings, and intentions. For young learners, understanding the nuances of body language is a key step in developing social awareness, empathy, and effective communication skills. It's a language that transcends words, allowing us to connect with others on a deeper level and navigate social situations with greater ease and confidence.

Imagine a child standing before a group of their peers, their shoulders hunched, their eyes downcast, their arms crossed defensively. This closed-off posture sends a clear message of insecurity and discomfort. Now, picture the same child standing tall, their head held high, their arms open and welcoming. This open posture exudes confidence and approachability, inviting others to engage with them. These two scenarios illustrate the profound impact that body language can have on our interactions with others.

The power of body language lies in its ability to convey emotions, intentions, and attitudes that may not be expressed verbally. When we interact with others, our bodies are constantly sending signals, often unconsciously. These signals can be as subtle as a raised eyebrow or as overt as a warm embrace. By paying attention to these nonverbal cues, we can gain valuable insights into the thoughts and feelings of others, even when they are not explicitly stated.

For children, learning to read and interpret body language is a crucial aspect of their social and emotional development. It is a skill that enables them to understand the unspoken messages in their interactions with others, to empathize with their feelings, and to respond appropriately. When children become aware of their own body language and how it affects others, they can use it to express themselves more effectively, build stronger relationships, and navigate social situations with greater ease.

The impact of body language extends beyond interpersonal interactions. In academic settings, nonverbal cues can influence how teachers perceive students and how students learn. A student who sits slouched in their chair with a bored expression may not be fully engaged in the lesson, while a student who leans forward with a look of interest is more likely to absorb the material. Teachers can use body language to gauge student understanding, provide feedback, and create a more engaging learning environment.

In the professional world, body language plays a crucial role in interviews, presentations, and networking events. A confident posture, a firm handshake, and good eye contact can create a positive first impression and convey professionalism and competence. Conversely, fidgeting, avoiding eye contact, and a slumped posture can signal insecurity and lack of interest.

The benefits of understanding body language are not limited to external achievements. On a personal level, awareness of nonverbal cues can enhance our relationships and deepen our connections with others. By paying attention to the subtle signals that our loved ones send through their body language, we can better understand their needs, respond with empathy, and strengthen our bonds.

Moreover, body language can be a powerful tool for self-expression and personal growth. By consciously adopting open and confident postures, we can boost our self-esteem and project a more positive image to the world. Similarly, by paying attention to our own nonverbal cues, we can gain valuable insights into our emotions, motivations, and unconscious biases.

Teaching children the importance of body language is a gift that will last a lifetime. It is a skill that will empower them to communicate more effectively, build stronger relationships, and navigate social situations with greater ease and confidence. By modeling positive body language, providing feedback, and creating opportunities for children to practice nonverbal communication, we can help them develop the social and emotional intelligence necessary for success in all areas of life.

In addition to the immediate benefits, understanding body language can have long-term implications for a child's personal and professional development. When children learn to read and interpret nonverbal cues, they are more likely to be seen as socially aware, empathetic, and emotionally intelligent. These qualities are highly valued in both personal and professional relationships and can open doors to opportunities in all areas of life.

Furthermore, body language can be a powerful tool for social change. When we use our bodies to express solidarity, protest injustice, or celebrate diversity, we are sending a message that is both powerful and undeniable. Children who learn to use their bodies to express their values and beliefs can become agents of change, advocating for a more just and equitable world.

In conclusion, body language is a universal language that speaks volumes about our thoughts, feelings, and intentions. For children, learning to read and interpret nonverbal cues is a vital step in developing social awareness, empathy, and effective communication skills. By nurturing this skill in our children, we are empowering them to connect with others on a deeper level, build stronger relationships, and navigate social situations with greater ease and confidence. So, let us all embrace the power of body language and use it to communicate with authenticity, compassion, and understanding.

ᗞᗞᗞ

Your body language speaks volumes, even when you're not saying a word. Stand tall, make eye contact, and use open gestures to project confidence and approachability. Your body is a powerful tool for communication, so use it wisely.

ELEVEN

LET'S TALK IT OUT! TALKING CAN SOLVE PROBLEMS

In the intricate tapestry of human relationships, conflicts and misunderstandings are inevitable. However, amidst these challenges lies an opportunity for growth, understanding, and resolution. The simple phrase "Let's talk it out" holds within it the transformative power of dialogue, offering a pathway to bridge differences, heal wounds, and find solutions that benefit all parties involved. For young learners, embracing this approach is not just a matter of conflict resolution; it is a life skill that fosters empathy, communication, and a collaborative spirit.

Imagine two friends engaged in a heated argument. Their voices rise, their words become sharp and accusatory, and the distance between them grows with each passing moment. But then, one of them takes a deep breath and utters those three simple words: "Let's talk it out." In that instant, the tension begins to dissipate, replaced by a glimmer of hope. The friends sit down, face to face, and begin to express their feelings, their perspectives, and their needs. As they talk, they listen to each other with open hearts and minds, seeking to understand rather than to judge. Through this dialogue, they discover common ground, find ways to compromise, and ultimately, strengthen their friendship.

The power of talking it out lies in its ability to create a safe and respectful space for open communication. When we engage in dialogue, we are not just expressing our own views but also actively listening to the perspectives of others. This exchange of ideas and feelings fosters understanding, empathy, and a willingness to find solutions that work for everyone.

For children, learning to talk it out is a crucial step in developing healthy relationships and conflict resolution skills. It is a skill that teaches them to express their needs and concerns in a constructive way, to listen to others with empathy and respect, and to work collaboratively to find solutions that benefit everyone. When children learn to talk it out, they are not only resolving conflicts but also building trust, strengthening relationships, and fostering a sense of community.

The impact of talking it out extends beyond interpersonal relationships. In academic settings, the ability to engage in constructive dialogue is essential for effective collaboration and knowledge sharing. Whether it's working on group projects, participating in class discussions, or engaging in debates, talking it out allows students to learn from each other, challenge each other's perspectives, and arrive at more nuanced and informed conclusions.

Furthermore, talking it out is a valuable asset in the professional world. Effective communication is a key ingredient for success in any career, and the ability to navigate conflict and negotiate win-win solutions is highly valued by employers. Children who learn to talk it out are more likely to excel in team collaborations, conflict resolution, and customer service.

The benefits of talking it out are not limited to external achievements. On a personal level, talking it out can improve our mental and emotional well-being. When we express our feelings and concerns openly and honestly, we are releasing pent-up emotions and reducing stress. This can lead to improved mental clarity, emotional regulation, and overall well-being.

Moreover, talking it out can strengthen our relationships and deepen our connections with others. When we engage in open and honest dialogue, we are building trust, fostering intimacy, and creating a space for mutual understanding and support. This can lead to stronger bonds, greater resilience, and a more fulfilling life.

Teaching children the importance of talking it out is a gift that will last a lifetime. It is a skill that will empower them to navigate conflict with grace and confidence, build strong relationships, and create a more peaceful and harmonious world. By modeling healthy communication skills, providing children with opportunities to practice dialogue in a safe and supportive environment, and encouraging them to express their feelings and needs openly, we can help them develop the communication skills necessary for success in all areas of life.

In addition to the immediate benefits, talking it out can have long-term implications for a child's personal and professional development. When children learn to communicate effectively, they are more likely to be seen as confident, assertive, and collaborative. These qualities can open doors to opportunities in both their personal and professional lives.

Furthermore, talking it out can be a powerful tool for social change. When we engage in dialogue with those who hold different views, we can challenge our own biases, expand our perspectives, and find common ground. This can lead to greater understanding, empathy, and cooperation, paving the way for a more just and equitable society.

In conclusion, the phrase "Let's talk it out" is more than just an invitation to conversation; it is a call to action, a commitment to finding solutions through open and honest dialogue. For children, learning to talk it out is a transformative journey that can lead to stronger relationships, greater self-awareness, and a more fulfilling life. By embracing the power of dialogue, we can create a world where conflict is not feared but embraced as an opportunity for growth, understanding, and connection. So, let us all commit to talking it out, for it is through dialogue that we can bridge our differences, heal our wounds, and create a more peaceful and harmonious world for ourselves and for generations to come.

ᗴᗴᗴ

When conflicts arise, choose dialogue over silence. Talking it out can lead to understanding, compromise, and stronger relationships. Remember, the most effective solutions are often found through open and honest communication.

TWELVE

STAND TALL! GOOD POSTURE SHOWS CONFIDENCE

In the intricate ballet of human expression, posture plays a leading role, often revealing more about our inner state than words ever could. From the confident stride of a leader to the slumped shoulders of someone burdened with worry, our bodies speak volumes through the silent language of posture. For young learners, understanding the significance of standing tall is not merely a matter of physical alignment; it is a gateway to self-assurance, empowerment, and the ability to command respect and attention.

Imagine a child walking into a room with their head held high, their shoulders back, and their spine straight. They exude an aura of confidence, their presence radiating positivity and strength. Now, picture the same child shuffling in with their head bowed, their shoulders hunched, and their eyes avoiding contact. This posture signals insecurity and self-doubt, diminishing their impact and presence. These contrasting scenarios highlight the profound influence that posture can have on our perception of ourselves and how others perceive us.

The power of standing tall lies in its ability to convey confidence, competence, and self-assurance. When we stand with good posture, we not only improve our physical alignment but also project a positive and powerful image to the world. This nonverbal cue communicates that we are capable, self-assured, and ready to take on challenges.

For children, learning to stand tall is a fundamental building block for developing self-esteem and confidence. It is a skill that empowers them to embrace their individuality, own their space, and project an image of self-assurance that can inspire others. When children stand tall, they are not only improving their physical well-being but also cultivating a sense of inner strength and resilience that can help them navigate life's challenges with greater ease.

The impact of good posture extends beyond personal presentation. Research has shown that standing tall can have a profound effect on our mental and emotional state. When we assume a confident posture, our brains release dopamine and serotonin, neurotransmitters associated with happiness, motivation, and well-being. This biochemical reaction not only makes us feel good but also enhances our cognitive function, improves our mood, and reduces stress levels.

In the context of communication, posture plays a crucial role in how our message is received. When we stand tall and speak with confidence, our words carry more weight and are perceived as more credible. This is because our body language reinforces our verbal message, signaling that we believe in what we are saying and that we are worthy of being heard. Conversely, poor posture can undermine our message, making us appear less confident and less convincing.

Furthermore, good posture can enhance our physical performance and well-being. When we stand with proper alignment, our muscles and joints are in their optimal position, reducing strain and improving our range of motion. This can lead to increased energy levels, improved athletic performance, and a reduced risk of injury. Good posture can also improve our breathing, digestion, and circulation, contributing to overall health and vitality.

Teaching children the importance of standing tall is a valuable investment in their future. It is a skill that can be nurtured and developed through practice, feedback, and encouragement. By modeling good posture, providing children with opportunities to engage in physical activities that promote strength and flexibility, and emphasizing the importance of self-care, we can help them cultivate a habit of standing tall that will benefit them throughout their lives.

In addition to the immediate benefits, standing tall can have long-term implications for a child's personal and professional development. When children learn to carry themselves with confidence, they are more likely to be seen as leaders, role models, and positive influences on others. This can open doors to opportunities in all areas of life, from academics and athletics to social interactions and career advancement.

Moreover, standing tall can be a powerful tool for personal transformation. By consciously adopting a confident posture, we can shift our mindset and overcome self-doubt. This act of self-empowerment can have a ripple effect, influencing our thoughts, feelings, and actions in a positive way.

In conclusion, the act of standing tall is more than just a physical stance; it is an expression of our inner strength, confidence, and resilience. For children, learning to stand tall is a fundamental skill that lays the foundation for a lifetime of self-assurance, empowerment, and success. By nurturing this skill in our children, we are not only improving their physical well-being but also cultivating a sense of inner strength and self-belief that will serve them well in all aspects of life. So, let us all stand tall, for our posture has the power to transform our lives and inspire others to do the same.

❦❦❦

Stand tall, not just physically but also in your beliefs and values. Good posture is a reflection of your inner confidence and self-assurance. When you stand tall, you show the world that you are ready to face any challenge.

THIRTEEN

DISAGREE RESPECTFULLY! IT'S OKAY TO HAVE DIFFERENT OPINIONS

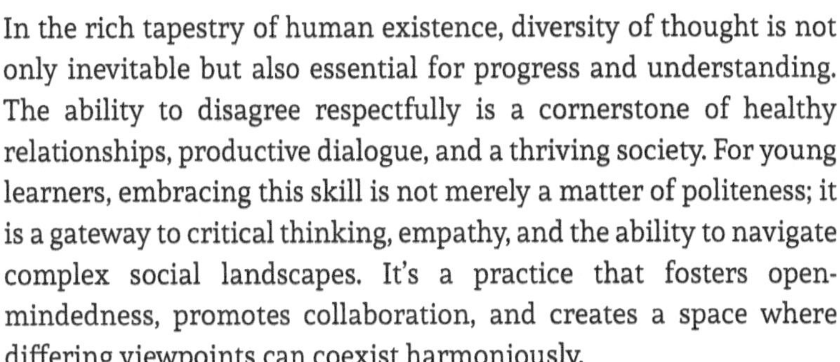

In the rich tapestry of human existence, diversity of thought is not only inevitable but also essential for progress and understanding. The ability to disagree respectfully is a cornerstone of healthy relationships, productive dialogue, and a thriving society. For young learners, embracing this skill is not merely a matter of politeness; it is a gateway to critical thinking, empathy, and the ability to navigate complex social landscapes. It's a practice that fosters open-mindedness, promotes collaboration, and creates a space where differing viewpoints can coexist harmoniously.

Imagine a group of friends gathered around a table, engaged in a lively discussion about their favorite sports teams. While some passionately advocate for their chosen team, others express their support for rival teams. Instead of devolving into a shouting match or resorting to personal attacks, the friends listen attentively to each other's arguments, acknowledge their differing perspectives, and engage in a respectful debate. This exchange of ideas, while filled with passion and conviction, remains respectful and constructive, ultimately strengthening their bonds and deepening their understanding of one another.

The power of disagreeing respectfully lies in its ability to transform conflict into an opportunity for growth and learning. When we approach disagreements with an open mind and a willingness to listen, we create a space where diverse perspectives can be shared and explored. This exchange of ideas can lead to new insights, creative solutions, and a deeper understanding of complex issues.

For children, learning to disagree respectfully is a crucial step in developing social and emotional intelligence. It is a skill that teaches them to value diversity, to appreciate different viewpoints, and to communicate their own opinions in a clear and respectful manner. When children learn to disagree respectfully, they are not only building strong relationships but also cultivating a sense of empathy, tolerance, and open-mindedness.

The impact of disagreeing respectfully extends beyond interpersonal interactions. In academic settings, the ability to engage in respectful debate is essential for critical thinking and intellectual growth. Whether it's analyzing historical events, discussing scientific theories, or interpreting literary texts, disagreeing respectfully allows students to challenge assumptions, explore different interpretations, and arrive at more nuanced and informed conclusions.

Furthermore, disagreeing respectfully is a valuable asset in the professional world. In today's globalized and interconnected society, we are increasingly working with people from diverse backgrounds and perspectives. The ability to navigate these differences with respect and understanding is essential for building strong teams, resolving conflicts, and achieving common goals.

The benefits of disagreeing respectfully are not limited to external achievements. On a personal level, embracing diverse opinions can enrich our lives and broaden our horizons. When we open ourselves up to different perspectives, we are challenged to question our own assumptions and beliefs, leading to greater self-awareness and personal growth. This openness can also lead to new friendships, collaborations, and opportunities for learning and development.

Teaching children the importance of disagreeing respectfully is a gift that will last a lifetime. It is a skill that will empower them to navigate conflict with grace and confidence, build strong relationships, and contribute to a more inclusive and tolerant society. By modeling respectful disagreement, providing children with opportunities to practice this skill in a safe and supportive environment, and encouraging them to express their opinions in a clear and respectful manner, we can help them develop the communication skills necessary for success in all areas of life.

In addition to the immediate benefits, disagreeing respectfully can have long-term implications for a child's personal and professional development. When children learn to communicate effectively and respectfully, they are more likely to be seen as thoughtful, open-minded, and collaborative. These qualities are highly valued in both personal and professional relationships and can open doors to opportunities in all areas of life.

Moreover, disagreeing respectfully can be a powerful tool for social change. When we engage in dialogue with those who hold different views, we can challenge our own biases, expand our perspectives, and find common ground. This can lead to greater understanding, empathy, and cooperation, paving the way for a more just and equitable society.

In conclusion, the ability to disagree respectfully is a fundamental skill that is essential for healthy relationships, productive dialogue, and a thriving society. For children, learning to embrace diverse opinions and communicate their own views in a respectful manner is a journey of self-discovery, empathy, and growth. By fostering a culture of respect, open-mindedness, and constructive dialogue, we are empowering children to become thoughtful, engaged, and compassionate individuals who can make a positive impact on the world. So, let us all embrace the power of respectful disagreement and use it to build bridges, foster understanding, and create a more inclusive and harmonious society for ourselves and for generations to come.

ppp

It's okay to have different opinions, but always remember to express them with respect. Disagreements can be opportunities for growth and learning, as long as we approach them with open minds and a willingness to listen.

FOURTEEN

Say "Thank You"! Gratitude Makes Everyone Happy

In the intricate tapestry of human interaction, gratitude emerges as a radiant thread, weaving together threads of appreciation, kindness, and joy. The simple act of saying "thank you" is not merely a social nicety; it is a powerful expression of gratitude that has the potential to transform our relationships, our communities, and our own well-being.

For young learners, cultivating gratitude is not just a matter of good manners; it is a mindset that fosters happiness, resilience, and a deeper connection with the world around them.

Imagine a child receiving a gift from a loved one. Their eyes light up with excitement as they unwrap the present, their heart filled with joy and appreciation. With a genuine smile, they express their gratitude with two simple words: "Thank you." In that moment, a wave of warmth washes over both the giver and the receiver, solidifying their bond and creating a shared sense of happiness.

The power of gratitude lies in its ability to shift our focus from what we lack to what we have. When we express gratitude, we are acknowledging the kindness, generosity, and support that we receive from others. This recognition not only strengthens our relationships but also cultivates a sense of abundance and contentment within ourselves.

For children, learning to say "thank you" is a fundamental step in developing empathy and social awareness. It is a skill that teaches them to value the contributions of others, to appreciate the little things in life, and to express their gratitude in a sincere and meaningful way. When children say "thank you," they are not only acknowledging the kindness they have received but also reinforcing positive behaviors in those around them.

The impact of gratitude extends beyond the individual. Research has shown that gratitude can have a profound effect on our physical and mental health. When we practice gratitude, our brains release dopamine and serotonin, neurotransmitters associated with happiness, well-being, and resilience. Gratitude has also been linked to lower levels of stress, anxiety, and depression, as well as improved sleep, stronger immune function, and greater overall life satisfaction.

In the context of relationships, gratitude serves as a powerful tool for building trust, deepening connections, and fostering positive interactions. When we express our gratitude to others, we are acknowledging their efforts and validating their contributions.

This act of recognition can strengthen our bonds with them and create a virtuous cycle of appreciation and goodwill.

Furthermore, gratitude is not just about feeling good; it is also about acting in ways that benefit ourselves and others. Research has shown that grateful people are more likely to help others, volunteer their time, and engage in prosocial behaviors. This suggests that gratitude is not only a source of personal happiness but also a catalyst for creating a more compassionate and supportive society.

Teaching children the importance of saying "thank you" is a valuable life skill that can benefit them in countless ways. It is a skill that can help them build stronger relationships, develop resilience in the face of adversity, and cultivate a positive outlook on life.

By modeling gratitude, encouraging children to express their appreciation, and creating opportunities for them to practice gratitude in their daily lives, we can help them unlock the transformative power of this simple yet profound emotion.

In addition to the immediate benefits, gratitude can have long-term implications for a child's personal and professional development. When children learn to appreciate the contributions of others and express their gratitude, they are more likely to be seen as kind, compassionate, and grateful individuals.

These qualities are highly valued in both personal and professional relationships and can open doors to opportunities in all areas of life.

Moreover, gratitude can be a powerful tool for personal growth and self-awareness. When we take the time to reflect on the things we are grateful for, we are shifting our focus from what we lack to what we have. This shift in perspective can help us appreciate the present moment, cultivate a sense of abundance, and find joy in the simple things in life.

In conclusion, the act of saying "thank you" is more than just a polite gesture; it is a powerful expression of gratitude that can transform our lives and the lives of those around us. For children, learning to cultivate gratitude is a journey of self-discovery, empathy, and connection.

By encouraging children to express their appreciation and practice gratitude in their daily lives, we are empowering them to lead happier, healthier, and more fulfilling lives. So, let us all embrace the power of gratitude and use it to create a more joyful, compassionate, and interconnected world for ourselves and for generations to come.

ᐅᐅᐅ

Saying "thank you" is a simple act of gratitude that can have a profound impact. It shows appreciation, builds trust, and strengthens relationships. Remember, gratitude is the key to happiness.

FIFTEEN

APOLOGIZE WHEN YOU NEED TO! SAYING SORRY SHOWS YOU CARE

In the intricate tapestry of human relationships, mistakes and misunderstandings are inevitable. However, amidst these challenges lies an opportunity for growth, healing, and reconciliation. The simple act of apologizing, when done with sincerity and empathy, holds within it the transformative power to mend broken bridges, rebuild trust, and restore harmony. For young learners, embracing the practice of apology is not just a matter of etiquette; it is a life skill that fosters humility, compassion, and accountability. It's a gesture that demonstrates a willingness to take responsibility for our actions, acknowledge the impact of our mistakes on others, and seek forgiveness.

Imagine a child accidentally bumping into another child on the playground, causing them to fall and scrape their knee. The child who caused the mishap feels a pang of guilt and remorse, their heart sinking as they see the tears welling up in the other child's eyes. With a trembling voice, they utter a heartfelt apology: "I'm so sorry." In that moment, a wave of relief washes over both children. The injured child feels acknowledged and comforted, while the apologetic child experiences a sense of release and renewed connection.

The power of apologizing lies in its ability to acknowledge and validate the feelings of others. When we apologize, we are not just saying words; we are communicating that we understand the impact of our actions on others and that we take responsibility for the pain we have caused. This act of empathy and accountability can be incredibly healing, as it allows the injured party to feel seen, heard, and valued.

For children, learning to apologize is a crucial step in developing emotional intelligence and healthy relationships. It is a skill that teaches them to take ownership of their mistakes, to empathize with the feelings of others, and to make amends for their wrongdoing. When children learn to apologize sincerely, they are not only repairing damaged relationships but also building trust, respect, and a sense of accountability.

The impact of apologizing goes beyond interpersonal relationships. In academic settings, the ability to apologize for mistakes and learn from them is essential for growth and development. When students are able to acknowledge their errors, they are more likely to take responsibility for their learning, seek help when needed, and persevere in the face of challenges.

Furthermore, apologizing is a valuable asset in the professional world. In the workplace, mistakes are inevitable, and the ability to apologize sincerely and take corrective action is crucial for maintaining trust and credibility. Employees who are able to apologize for their errors and learn from them are more likely to be seen as responsible, reliable, and accountable.

The benefits of apologizing are not limited to external achievements. On a personal level, apologizing can free us from the burden of guilt and shame. When we acknowledge our mistakes and take responsibility for them, we are able to move forward with a clear conscience and a renewed sense of integrity. Apologizing can also help us to forgive ourselves, fostering self-compassion and promoting emotional healing.

Moreover, apologizing can strengthen our relationships and deepen our connections with others. When we apologize sincerely, we are demonstrating humility, empathy, and a willingness to repair the damage we have caused. This act of vulnerability can create a space for forgiveness, reconciliation, and a renewed sense of trust.

Teaching children the importance of apologizing is a gift that will last a lifetime. It is a skill that will empower them to navigate conflict with grace and compassion, build strong relationships, and make amends for their mistakes. By modeling sincere apologies, providing children with opportunities to practice apologizing in a safe and supportive environment, and encouraging them to take responsibility for their actions, we can help them develop the communication skills necessary for healthy and fulfilling relationships.

In addition to the immediate benefits, apologizing can have long-term implications for a child's personal and professional development. When children learn to apologize sincerely and take responsibility for their actions, they are more likely to be seen as trustworthy, reliable, and compassionate. These qualities are highly valued in both personal and professional relationships and can open doors to opportunities in all areas of life.

Furthermore, apologizing can be a powerful tool for social change. When we are willing to acknowledge the harm we have caused and take steps to make amends, we are contributing to a more just and equitable society. Children who learn to apologize sincerely can become agents of change, promoting healing, reconciliation, and forgiveness in their communities.

In conclusion, the act of apologizing is more than just a gesture of politeness; it is a powerful tool for healing, reconciliation, and growth. For children, learning to apologize is a journey of self-awareness, empathy, and accountability. By encouraging children to apologize sincerely and take responsibility for their actions, we are empowering them to build stronger relationships, navigate conflict with grace, and become compassionate and responsible members of society. So, let us all embrace the power of apology and use it to heal wounds, mend broken bridges, and create a more forgiving and compassionate world for ourselves and for generations to come.

$$\triangleright\triangleright\triangleright$$

When you make a mistake, don't be afraid to say, "I'm sorry." Apologizing is a sign of strength and shows that you care about the feelings of others. Remember, a sincere apology can mend broken bridges and restore trust.

SIXTEEN

BE A GOOD LISTENER! EVERYONE WANTS TO FEEL HEARD

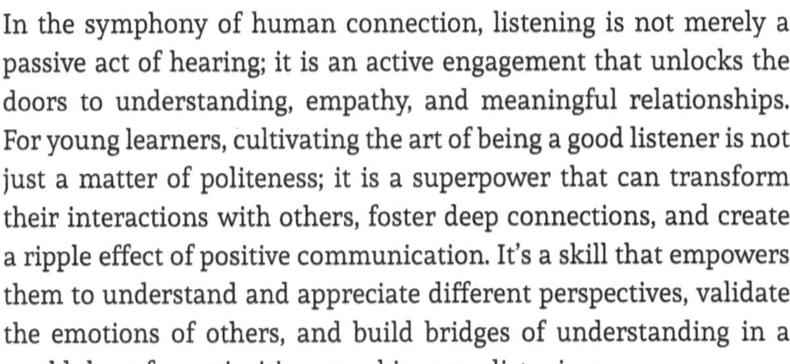

In the symphony of human connection, listening is not merely a passive act of hearing; it is an active engagement that unlocks the doors to understanding, empathy, and meaningful relationships. For young learners, cultivating the art of being a good listener is not just a matter of politeness; it is a superpower that can transform their interactions with others, foster deep connections, and create a ripple effect of positive communication. It's a skill that empowers them to understand and appreciate different perspectives, validate the emotions of others, and build bridges of understanding in a world that often prioritizes speaking over listening.

Imagine a child sitting beside a friend who is visibly upset. Instead of interrupting with advice or distractions, the child listens patiently, their eyes filled with concern and understanding. They nod their head gently, offering a comforting hand or a reassuring hug. As the friend pours out their heart, the listener absorbs their words, not just with their ears but with their entire being. This act of deep listening creates a safe space where the friend feels heard, understood, and validated.

The power of listening lies in its ability to create a profound sense of connection and empathy. When we truly listen to another person, we are not just hearing their words; we are entering their world, experiencing their emotions, and understanding their perspective. This act of empathy fosters trust, deepens relationships, and opens the door for genuine communication.

For children, learning to be a good listener is a fundamental skill that underpins all aspects of their social and emotional development. It is a skill that enables them to build strong relationships, resolve conflicts peacefully, and navigate complex social situations with grace and compassion. When children learn to listen attentively, they are not only gaining valuable insights into the thoughts and feelings of others but also developing their own capacity for empathy and understanding.

The impact of listening goes beyond interpersonal relationships. In academic settings, the ability to listen actively is crucial for learning and knowledge acquisition. Whether it's listening to a teacher's lecture, participating in a group discussion, or collaborating on a project, good listening skills enable students to absorb information, make connections, and develop a deeper understanding of the subject matter.

Furthermore, listening is a valuable asset in the professional world. Effective communication is a key ingredient for success in any career, and the ability to listen attentively to clients, colleagues, and superiors is essential for building rapport, resolving conflicts, and achieving common goals. Children who learn to listen well are more likely to excel in teamwork, negotiation, and customer service.

The benefits of being a good listener are not limited to external achievements. On a personal level, listening can enrich our lives and deepen our connections with others. When we truly listen to our loved ones, we are showing them that we value their thoughts, feelings, and experiences. This act of validation can strengthen our bonds with them and foster a sense of mutual respect and understanding.

Moreover, listening can be a powerful tool for personal growth and self-awareness. By listening attentively to our own inner voice, we can gain valuable insights into our emotions, motivations, and values. This self-awareness can guide us in making decisions that are aligned with our authentic selves and lead to a more fulfilling life.

Teaching children the importance of being a good listener is a gift that will last a lifetime. It is a skill that will empower them to build stronger relationships, resolve conflicts peacefully, and navigate social situations with grace and compassion. By modeling active listening, providing children with opportunities to practice listening skills in a safe and supportive environment, and encouraging them to be curious and open-minded, we can help them develop the communication skills necessary for success in all areas of life.

In addition to the immediate benefits, being a good listener can have long-term implications for a child's personal and professional development. When children learn to listen attentively and empathetically, they are more likely to be seen as trustworthy, approachable, and compassionate. These qualities are highly valued in both personal and professional relationships and can open doors to opportunities in all areas of life.

Furthermore, listening can be a powerful tool for social change. When we truly listen to the voices of those who are marginalized or oppressed, we are amplifying their stories, validating their experiences, and creating space for their perspectives to be heard. Children who learn to listen with empathy and compassion can become powerful advocates for social justice and change.

In conclusion, the act of listening is a profound gift that we can give to ourselves and others. It is a skill that empowers us to connect with others on a deeper level, to understand their perspectives, and to foster empathy and compassion. For children, learning to be a good listener is a journey of self-discovery, relationship building, and personal growth. By nurturing this skill in our children, we are not only giving them the tools to succeed but also empowering them to become compassionate, empathetic, and effective communicators who can make a positive impact on the world. So, let us all embrace the power of listening and use it to create a more understanding, inclusive, and harmonious world for ourselves and for generations to come.

ϷϷϷ

Be present when others speak. Truly listen, not just to their words, but also to their feelings. Everyone deserves to feel heard and understood.

SEVENTEEN

GIVE COMPLIMENTS! KIND WORDS MAKE PEOPLE SMILE

In the intricate dance of human interaction, words possess a remarkable power to uplift, inspire, and forge connections. The simple act of giving a compliment, when offered with sincerity and warmth, can brighten someone's day, boost their confidence, and leave a lasting positive impact. For young learners, mastering the art of giving compliments is not just a matter of etiquette; it is a profound expression of kindness and appreciation that nurtures relationships, fosters empathy, and creates a ripple effect of joy and goodwill.

Imagine a child noticing a classmate's new haircut and taking a moment to express their admiration. "Your hair looks amazing!" they exclaim with a genuine smile. In that instant, a spark of happiness ignites in the classmate's eyes, their cheeks flushing with warmth and pride. This simple compliment, offered without hesitation or ulterior motive, has the power to transform the recipient's day, boosting their self-esteem and making them feel seen and valued.

The power of compliments lies in their ability to acknowledge and celebrate the unique qualities, strengths, and efforts of others. When we offer a compliment, we are not just saying words; we are communicating that we see and appreciate the person for who they are, recognizing their inherent worth and value. This act of affirmation can have a profound effect on a person's self-perception, fostering a sense of confidence, belonging, and positive self-worth.

For children, learning to give compliments is a fundamental step in developing empathy and social awareness. It is a skill that teaches them to recognize and appreciate the positive qualities in others, to express their admiration in a genuine and heartfelt way, and to build bridges of connection through positive reinforcement. When children give compliments, they are not only spreading joy and goodwill but also strengthening their own relationships and creating a more positive and supportive social environment.

The impact of compliments extends far beyond the immediate moment of interaction. Research has shown that receiving compliments can trigger the release of dopamine, a neurotransmitter associated with pleasure, reward, and motivation. This biochemical reaction not only makes us feel good but also reinforces positive behaviors, encourages personal growth, and strengthens our sense of self-efficacy.

In the context of relationships, compliments serve as a powerful tool for building rapport, expressing appreciation, and strengthening bonds. When we offer compliments to our loved ones, friends, and colleagues, we are communicating that we value their presence in our lives and appreciate their unique contributions. This act of recognition can deepen our connections with others, foster mutual respect, and create a more positive and supportive social environment.

Furthermore, compliments are not just about making others feel good; they are also about effective communication. When we offer compliments, we are providing positive feedback that can help others to identify their strengths, recognize their achievements, and build confidence in their abilities. This type of feedback can be particularly valuable for children who are still developing their sense of self and may be unsure of their strengths and talents.

Teaching children the art of giving compliments is a gift that will last a lifetime. It is a skill that will empower them to build stronger relationships, foster a more positive and supportive social environment, and contribute to a world where kindness and appreciation are valued. By modeling the act of giving compliments, encouraging children to express their appreciation for others, and providing them with opportunities to practice this skill, we can help them cultivate a habit of kindness and appreciation that will enrich their lives and the lives of those around them.

In addition to the immediate benefits, giving compliments can have long-term implications for a child's personal and professional development. When children learn to recognize and appreciate the positive qualities in others, they are more likely to be seen as kind, compassionate, and supportive individuals. These qualities are highly valued in both personal and professional relationships and can open doors to opportunities in all areas of life.

Moreover, giving compliments can be a powerful tool for personal growth and self-awareness. When we make a conscious effort to look for the good in others and express our appreciation, we are also cultivating a more positive and optimistic outlook on life. This shift in perspective can help us to focus on the abundance in our own lives, leading to greater happiness, contentment, and well-being.

In conclusion, the act of giving a compliment is more than just a polite gesture; it is a profound expression of kindness and appreciation that can transform our relationships, our communities, and our own lives. For children, learning to give compliments is a journey of empathy, social awareness, and personal growth. By nurturing this skill in our children, we are empowering them to create a more positive and supportive world, one compliment at a time. So, let us all embrace the power of compliments and use them to uplift others, spread joy, and make the world a brighter place.

ᗬᗬᗬ

Spread kindness with your words. A compliment, a word of encouragement, or a simple "thank you" can brighten someone's day and create a ripple effect of positivity.

EIGHTEEN

TELL JOKES! LAUGHTER BRINGS PEOPLE TOGETHER

In the symphony of human interaction, laughter is a joyous melody that transcends cultural barriers, age differences, and social status. It is a universal language that speaks to the heart, fostering connection, joy, and a shared sense of humanity. For young learners, embracing the art of telling jokes is not merely a matter of amusement; it is a powerful tool for building relationships, diffusing tension, and creating a positive and inclusive social environment. It's a skill that cultivates a sense of humor, promotes lightheartedness, and strengthens the bonds between individuals, reminding us that even in the face of challenges, laughter can bring us together and uplift our spirits.

Imagine a group of children gathered in a circle, their faces beaming with laughter as they share jokes and funny stories. The air is filled with infectious giggles and playful banter, creating a warm and welcoming atmosphere. In that moment, the children are not just sharing jokes; they are building connections, forging friendships, and creating memories that will last a lifetime.

The power of laughter lies in its ability to break down barriers and create a sense of shared experience. When we laugh together, we are not just reacting to a humorous situation; we are experiencing a moment of connection and joy. This shared experience can be incredibly powerful, as it transcends our individual differences and unites us in a common bond.

For children, learning to tell jokes is a valuable skill that can enhance their social and emotional development. It is a skill that teaches them to be playful, creative, and spontaneous. When children tell jokes, they are not only entertaining others but also expressing themselves in a unique and engaging way. This can boost their confidence, improve their communication skills, and help them connect with others on a deeper level.

The impact of laughter goes beyond social interactions. Research has shown that laughter has numerous physical and mental health benefits. When we laugh, our bodies release endorphins, natural mood boosters that can reduce stress, alleviate pain, and boost our immune system. Laughter has also been linked to improved cardiovascular health, enhanced cognitive function, and increased creativity.

In the context of relationships, laughter serves as a powerful tool for building rapport, diffusing tension, and strengthening bonds. When we share a laugh with someone, we are creating a shared experience that can foster intimacy, trust, and connection. This can be particularly important for children who are still developing their social skills and may feel hesitant or shy in new situations. Telling a joke can break the ice, create a sense of camaraderie, and open the door for deeper conversations and connections.

Furthermore, laughter is not just about amusement; it is also a form of communication. Jokes often contain subtle social commentary, cultural references, or observations about human nature. By understanding and appreciating humor, children can develop a deeper understanding of the world around them and the complexities of human interaction.

Teaching children the art of telling jokes is a gift that will last a lifetime. It is a skill that will empower them to bring joy to others, navigate social situations with ease, and build lasting connections. By encouraging children to explore their sense of humor, share funny stories, and create their own jokes, we are fostering their creativity, communication skills, and overall well-being.

In addition to the immediate benefits, telling jokes can have long-term implications for a child's personal and professional development. When children learn to use humor effectively, they are more likely to be seen as approachable, likable, and charismatic. These qualities can open doors to opportunities in all areas of life, from friendships and romantic relationships to career advancement and leadership roles.

Moreover, laughter can be a powerful tool for social change. Humor can be used to challenge stereotypes, expose injustice, and inspire action. Children who learn to use humor to address serious issues can become powerful advocates for positive change, using their wit and creativity to raise awareness, spark conversations, and mobilize communities.

In conclusion, the act of telling jokes is more than just a way to make people laugh; it is a powerful tool for building connections, fostering joy, and promoting social change. For children, learning to tell jokes is a journey of self-expression, creativity, and connection. By encouraging children to embrace their sense of humor and share it with others, we are empowering them to become more confident, empathetic, and joyful individuals who can make a positive impact on the world. So, let us all embrace the power of laughter and use it to spread joy, build bridges, and create a more connected and compassionate world.

♥♥♥

Laughter is a universal language that connects us all. Tell jokes, share funny stories, and don't be afraid to be silly. Laughter brings joy, relieves stress, and strengthens bonds.

NINETEEN

BE YOURSELF! THE BEST WAY TO CONNECT IS TO BE GENUINE

In the grand tapestry of human relationships, authenticity shines as a beacon of truth, fostering genuine connections that transcend superficiality and artifice. For young learners, embracing their true selves is not just a matter of self-acceptance; it is a superpower that unlocks the door to meaningful relationships, personal growth, and a fulfilling life. It's a journey of self-discovery, courage, and vulnerability, where the masks we wear are shed, revealing the unique and beautiful individuals we are meant to be.

Imagine a child standing on a stage, their heart pounding as they prepare to perform a talent they are not passionate about, simply to please others. Their movements are stiff, their expression forced, and their performance lacks the spark of genuine enthusiasm. Now, picture the same child on a different stage, their face alight with joy as they share a talent they truly love. Their movements are fluid, their expression genuine, and their performance radiates with passion and authenticity. These contrasting scenarios highlight the transformative power of being true to oneself.

The power of authenticity lies in its ability to foster genuine connections. When we are authentic, we are not trying to be someone we are not; we are embracing our true selves, with all our quirks, strengths, and vulnerabilities. This act of self-acceptance not only frees us from the burden of pretending but also invites others to connect with us on a deeper level.

For children, learning to be themselves is a crucial step in developing self-esteem, confidence, and healthy relationships. It is a journey that involves recognizing their unique qualities, embracing their differences, and expressing themselves authentically. When children feel safe to be themselves, they are more likely to form genuine connections with others, based on mutual respect, understanding, and acceptance.

The impact of authenticity extends beyond interpersonal relationships. In academic settings, the ability to be oneself can foster a more positive and inclusive learning environment. When students feel comfortable expressing their unique perspectives and ideas, they are more likely to participate in class discussions, engage in creative projects, and develop a deeper understanding of the subject matter.

Furthermore, authenticity is a valuable asset in the professional world. In an era where personal branding and online presence are increasingly important, the ability to present oneself authentically can set individuals apart from the crowd. Authentic leaders inspire trust, loyalty, and engagement, while authentic brands resonate with consumers on a deeper level.

The benefits of being yourself are not limited to external achievements. On a personal level, authenticity can lead to greater self-acceptance, self-love, and overall well-being. When we embrace our true selves, we are no longer burdened by the need to conform to societal expectations or to please others at the expense of our own happiness. This liberation can lead to greater self-confidence, inner peace, and a more fulfilling life.

Moreover, authenticity can foster deeper and more meaningful relationships. When we are genuine with others, we create a space for vulnerability, trust, and intimacy. This allows us to connect with others on a soul level, sharing our joys, sorrows, and dreams in a way that is both authentic and empowering.

Teaching children the importance of being themselves is a gift that will last a lifetime. It is a lesson that will empower them to embrace their individuality, pursue their passions, and live a life that is true to their values and beliefs. By modeling authenticity, encouraging children to express their unique personalities, and celebrating their differences, we can help them cultivate a sense of self-acceptance and confidence that will serve them well in all areas of life.

In addition to the immediate benefits, being yourself can have long-term implications for a child's personal and professional development. When children learn to embrace their true selves, they are more likely to be seen as confident, creative, and authentic individuals. These qualities are highly valued in both personal and professional relationships and can open doors to opportunities in all areas of life.

Furthermore, authenticity can be a powerful tool for social change. When we are brave enough to be ourselves, even in the face of adversity or criticism, we are challenging societal norms and paving the way for greater acceptance and inclusion. Children who learn to be themselves can become role models for others, inspiring them to embrace their own unique identities and live a life that is true to their hearts.

In conclusion, the journey of being yourself is a lifelong adventure, filled with challenges, triumphs, and endless possibilities. For children, learning to embrace their true selves is a fundamental step in developing self-esteem, confidence, and meaningful relationships. By nurturing authenticity in our children, we are empowering them to live a life that is rich, fulfilling, and true to their hearts. So, let us all embrace the power of authenticity and encourage our children to be themselves, for it is in our unique individuality that we find our greatest strength and our deepest connections with others.

ppp

Embrace your unique qualities, interests, and passions. The best way to connect with others is to be yourself. When you are authentic, you attract people who appreciate you for who you truly are.

TWENTY
Use Your Imagination! Tell Stories and Share Your Ideas

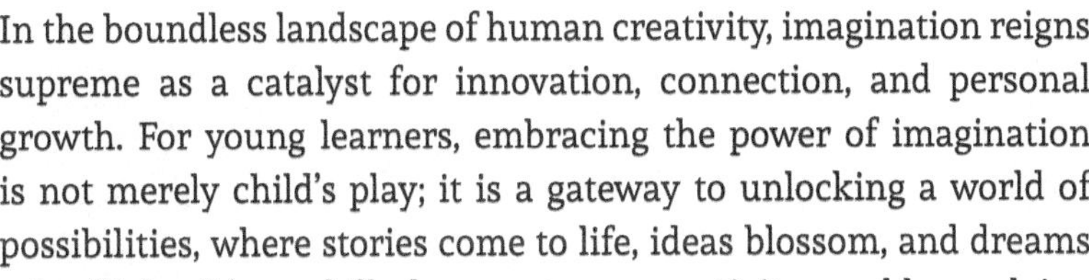

In the boundless landscape of human creativity, imagination reigns supreme as a catalyst for innovation, connection, and personal growth. For young learners, embracing the power of imagination is not merely child's play; it is a gateway to unlocking a world of possibilities, where stories come to life, ideas blossom, and dreams take flight. It's a skill that nurtures creativity, problem-solving abilities, and a sense of wonder, empowering them to express themselves, connect with others, and shape the world around them.

Imagine a child sitting on a grassy hilltop, their eyes twinkling with delight as they recount a fantastical tale of dragons, princesses, and magical quests. With each word, their audience is transported to a world of wonder and excitement, their imaginations ignited by the vivid imagery and captivating narrative. In that moment, the child is not just telling a story; they are creating an experience, forging a connection with their listeners, and sharing a glimpse of their inner world.

The power of storytelling and idea sharing lies in their ability to transcend the boundaries of reality and transport us to new and uncharted territories. When we share our stories and ideas, we are not just communicating information; we are inviting others to join us on a journey of exploration, discovery, and imagination. This shared experience can be incredibly powerful, as it fosters empathy, understanding, and a sense of connection that transcends our individual differences.

For children, using their imagination to tell stories and share ideas is a natural and essential part of their development. It is a way for them to make sense of the world around them, to explore their emotions, and to connect with others on a deeper level. When children are encouraged to use their imagination, they are not only developing their creativity and communication skills but also cultivating a sense of wonder and possibility that can last a lifetime.

The impact of storytelling and idea sharing extends beyond personal expression. In academic settings, the ability to articulate ideas clearly and creatively is essential for success. Whether it's writing essays, giving presentations, or participating in group discussions, students who can tap into their imagination and share their ideas in a compelling way are more likely to engage their audience and make a lasting impression.

Furthermore, imagination and idea sharing are critical skills in the professional world. In an era of rapid technological advancement and constant innovation, the ability to generate and communicate creative ideas is highly valued. Employees who can think outside the box, envision new possibilities, and share their ideas with passion and clarity are more likely to be seen as leaders and innovators.

The benefits of using imagination are not limited to external achievements. On a personal level, imagination can enrich our lives and enhance our well-being. When we allow ourselves to dream, to explore new ideas, and to create, we are tapping into a source of joy, fulfillment, and purpose. This can lead to greater self-awareness, personal growth, and a more meaningful life.

Moreover, imagination can be a powerful tool for problem-solving and conflict resolution. When we approach challenges with an open mind and a willingness to explore creative solutions, we are more likely to find innovative ways to overcome obstacles and achieve our goals. Similarly, when we use our imagination to put ourselves in the shoes of others, we can develop greater empathy and understanding, paving the way for more compassionate and collaborative relationships.

Teaching children the importance of using their imagination is a gift that will last a lifetime. It is a skill that will empower them to express themselves, connect with others, and create a more vibrant and meaningful world. By encouraging children to tell stories, share ideas, and explore their creative potential, we are nurturing their imagination, fostering their self-expression, and setting them on a path towards a fulfilling and creative life.

In addition to the immediate benefits, using imagination can have long-term implications for a child's personal and professional development. When children learn to think creatively, they are more likely to be seen as innovative, adaptable, and resourceful. These qualities are highly valued in both personal and professional relationships and can open doors to opportunities in all areas of life.

Furthermore, imagination can be a powerful tool for social change. When we use our imagination to envision a better future, we are inspiring ourselves and others to take action and create a more just, equitable, and sustainable world. Children who learn to use their imagination to dream big and envision a better future can become catalysts for positive change, creating a ripple effect that can transform our world.

In conclusion, the act of using imagination is a transformative force that can unlock our full potential, both individually and collectively. For children, imagination is a precious gift, a boundless source of creativity, joy, and connection. By nurturing this gift in our children, we are empowering them to become confident, creative, and compassionate individuals who can make a positive impact on the world. So, let us all embrace the power of imagination and use it to tell stories, share ideas, and create a more vibrant, meaningful, and hopeful future for ourselves and for generations to come.

Your imagination is a powerful tool for creativity and innovation. Use it to tell stories, share ideas, and explore new possibilities. Let your imagination soar, and watch your world expand.

TWENTY-ONE

PRACTICE MAKES PERFECT! THE MORE YOU TALK, THE EASIER IT GETS

In the vast landscape of human communication, the path to mastery is paved with practice. The simple adage "practice makes perfect" rings true in all aspects of life, and communication is no exception. For young learners, embracing the journey of practicing communication skills is not just a means to an end; it is a transformative process that builds confidence, competence, and a deep appreciation for the power of language. It's a commitment to continuous improvement, a willingness to step outside one's comfort zone, and a recognition that the more we engage in the art of conversation, the more natural and effortless it becomes.

Imagine a child learning to ride a bicycle. Their first attempts are wobbly and hesitant, filled with stumbles and falls. But with each ride, their balance improves, their confidence grows, and their movements become smoother and more coordinated. Similarly, a child's journey in mastering communication skills begins with tentative steps and awkward pauses. However, with consistent practice, their words flow more easily, their ideas become clearer, and their interactions with others become more meaningful and enjoyable.

The power of practice lies in its ability to strengthen neural pathways and create new habits. When we engage in repetitive activities, our brains adapt and learn, making the tasks easier and more automatic over time. This applies to communication skills as well. The more we practice speaking, listening, and expressing ourselves, the more fluent and confident we become in our interactions with others.

For children, practicing communication skills is a vital aspect of their social and emotional development. It is a process that involves learning to articulate their thoughts and feelings, to listen actively and empathetically, and to navigate complex social situations with grace and confidence. When children practice communication skills, they are not only honing their verbal and nonverbal abilities but also developing essential life skills such as problem-solving, conflict resolution, and relationship building.

The impact of practice extends beyond individual interactions. In academic settings, the practice of communication skills is essential for success. Whether it's participating in class discussions, presenting research findings, or collaborating on group projects, students who have honed their communication skills are better equipped to articulate their ideas, engage with their peers, and achieve their academic goals.

Furthermore, practice is a key ingredient for success in the professional world. Effective communication is a highly sought-after skill in any industry, and employers value individuals who can express themselves clearly, listen actively, and build strong relationships with colleagues and clients. Children who have practiced communication skills from a young age are more likely to thrive in job interviews, presentations, and team collaborations.

The benefits of practice are not limited to external achievements. On a personal level, practicing communication skills can lead to greater self-awareness, self-confidence, and overall well-being. When we communicate effectively, we are able to express our needs, desires, and opinions with clarity and conviction. This can lead to a stronger sense of self, improved self-esteem, and a more positive outlook on life.

Moreover, practicing communication skills can deepen our connections with others and enrich our relationships. When we are able to communicate openly and honestly with our loved ones, friends, and colleagues, we create a space for trust, intimacy, and mutual understanding. This can lead to stronger bonds, greater support, and a more fulfilling life.

Teaching children the importance of practice is a gift that will last a lifetime. It is a lesson that will empower them to embrace challenges, persevere in the face of setbacks, and achieve their full potential. By modeling the practice of communication skills, providing children with opportunities to practice in a safe and supportive environment, and celebrating their progress along the way, we can help them develop the communication skills necessary for success in all areas of life.

In addition to the immediate benefits, practicing communication skills can have long-term implications for a child's personal and professional development. When children learn to communicate effectively, they are more likely to be seen as confident, articulate, and persuasive. These qualities are highly valued in both personal and professional relationships and can open doors to opportunities in all areas of life.

Furthermore, the practice of communication skills can be a powerful tool for social change. When we are able to communicate effectively with people from diverse backgrounds and perspectives, we can bridge divides, build understanding, and create a more inclusive and equitable society. Children who have practiced communication skills from a young age are more likely to become engaged citizens who actively participate in civic discourse and work towards a better future for all.

In conclusion, the journey of mastering communication skills is a lifelong endeavor that requires dedication, patience, and a willingness to embrace the learning process. For children, practicing communication skills is a transformative experience that can build confidence, competence, and a deep appreciation for the power of language. By nurturing this skill in our children, we are empowering them to become effective communicators, compassionate individuals, and active contributors to society. So, let us all embrace the power of practice and encourage our children to explore the vast and wondrous world of human communication.

ᗐᗐᗐ

The more you practice communicating, the easier and more natural it will become. Don't be afraid to make mistakes, for they are stepping stones to growth and learning.

TWENTY-TWO

DON'T GIVE UP!
KEEP TRYING, EVEN
WHEN IT'S HARD

In the grand tapestry of life, challenges and setbacks are inevitable. From the minor frustrations of everyday life to the major obstacles that threaten to derail our dreams, adversity is an integral part of the human experience. However, within these challenges lies an opportunity for growth, resilience, and the discovery of our own inner strength. The simple phrase "Don't give up" encapsulates a profound message of perseverance, determination, and the unwavering belief in our ability to overcome adversity. It is a mantra that has inspired countless individuals throughout history, reminding us that even in the darkest of times, there is always hope, and that with persistence and resilience, we can emerge stronger and wiser from our struggles.

Imagine a child struggling to learn a new skill, such as riding a bike or playing an instrument. Their initial attempts are met with frustration and disappointment, their progress slow and unsteady. But with each failed attempt, a flicker of determination ignites within them. They dust themselves off, gather their courage, and try again. With each subsequent effort, their skills improve, their confidence grows, and their belief in their own abilities solidifies. Eventually, they achieve their goal, not through sheer talent or luck, but through the unwavering refusal to give up.

The power of not giving up lies in its ability to tap into the resilience of the human spirit. When faced with challenges, our natural instinct may be to retreat, to seek comfort in the familiar, to avoid the pain of failure. However, by choosing to persevere, to push through the discomfort and uncertainty, we unlock a hidden reservoir of strength and determination within ourselves.

For children, learning to not give up is a crucial life skill that will serve them well in all areas of life. It is a skill that teaches them to embrace challenges as opportunities for growth, to learn from their mistakes, and to persevere in the face of setbacks. When children learn to not give up, they are not only developing resilience but also cultivating a growth mindset, a belief that their abilities can be developed through dedication and hard work.

The impact of not giving up extends beyond personal achievements. In academic settings, the ability to persevere in the face of challenges is essential for success. Students who are willing to put in the effort, seek help when needed, and learn from their mistakes are more likely to achieve their academic goals and develop a love of learning.

Furthermore, not giving up is a valuable asset in the professional world. In the workplace, setbacks and obstacles are inevitable. Employees who can bounce back from failures, learn from their mistakes, and adapt to changing circumstances are more likely to be seen as valuable assets and to advance in their careers.

The benefits of not giving up are not limited to external achievements. On a personal level, perseverance can lead to greater self-confidence, self-efficacy, and overall well-being. When we overcome challenges and achieve our goals, we feel a sense of accomplishment and pride, which can boost our self-esteem and reinforce our belief in our own abilities.

Moreover, not giving up can help us to develop a more positive and optimistic outlook on life. When we face adversity with courage and determination, we are less likely to feel overwhelmed or defeated. Instead, we are able to see challenges as opportunities for growth and learning, which can lead to greater resilience and a more positive outlook on life.

Teaching children the importance of not giving up is a gift that will last a lifetime. It is a lesson that will empower them to face challenges head-on, to persevere in the face of adversity, and to achieve their dreams. By modeling resilience, providing children with opportunities to overcome obstacles, and celebrating their efforts and achievements, we can help them cultivate a spirit of perseverance that will serve them well in all aspects of life.

In addition to the immediate benefits, not giving up can have long-term implications for a child's personal and professional development. When children learn to persevere, they are more likely to be seen as determined, resilient, and capable individuals. These qualities are highly valued in both personal and professional relationships and can open doors to opportunities in all areas of life.

Furthermore, not giving up can be a powerful tool for social change. When we refuse to give up on our dreams, our communities, or our world, we are demonstrating a commitment to creating a better future for ourselves and for generations to come. Children who learn to persevere in the face of adversity can become powerful agents of change, inspiring others with their courage, determination, and unwavering belief in the possibility of a brighter future.

In conclusion, the phrase "Don't give up" is a mantra that has the power to transform lives and inspire greatness. For children, learning to embrace challenges, to persevere in the face of setbacks, and to never give up on their dreams is a journey of self-discovery, resilience, and personal growth. By fostering a culture of perseverance, we are empowering children to become confident, capable, and compassionate individuals who can make a positive impact on the world. So, let us all embrace the power of perseverance and inspire our children to never give up, for it is through our struggles that we discover our true strength and achieve our greatest potential.

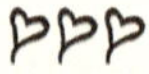

*When challenges arise, remember, "Don't give up!"
Perseverance and determination are the keys to
overcoming obstacles and achieving your dreams.*

TWENTY-THREE

ASK FOR HELP! IT'S OKAY TO NEED SUPPORT

In the complex tapestry of human existence, we are inherently social beings, wired to connect, collaborate, and rely on one another for support. Yet, the act of asking for help can often be fraught with fear, shame, and a misguided sense of self-sufficiency. For young learners, embracing the vulnerability of seeking assistance is not a sign of weakness; it is a testament to their courage, self-awareness, and understanding that no one can navigate life's challenges alone. It's a skill that fosters humility, builds resilience, and opens the door to a world of support, guidance, and shared learning.

Imagine a child struggling to complete a complex puzzle. Their frustration mounts as they try piece after piece, unable to find the perfect fit. They could continue to struggle in isolation, their pride preventing them from seeking help. However, with a deep breath and a courageous step, they turn to a friend or family member and ask for assistance. In that moment, a weight is lifted from their shoulders. Together, they examine the puzzle, share ideas, and eventually find the missing piece. The joy of collaborative problem-solving not only completes the puzzle but also strengthens the bond between them.

The power of asking for help lies in its ability to connect us with others and tap into a collective wisdom that far surpasses our individual capabilities. When we reach out for support, we are acknowledging that we don't have all the answers, that we need guidance and assistance to overcome challenges and achieve our goals. This act of vulnerability creates a space for collaboration, learning, and growth.

For children, learning to ask for help is a crucial step in developing social and emotional intelligence. It is a skill that teaches them to recognize their own limitations, to value the expertise and perspectives of others, and to build trusting relationships based on mutual support and understanding. When children learn to ask for help, they are not only overcoming challenges but also cultivating a sense of humility, resourcefulness, and connection.

The impact of asking for help extends beyond individual struggles. In academic settings, the ability to seek guidance from teachers, mentors, and peers is essential for academic success. Students who are willing to ask for help when they are struggling with a concept or assignment are more likely to understand the material, complete their work, and achieve their academic goals.

Furthermore, asking for help is a valuable asset in the professional world. In today's fast-paced and complex work environment, collaboration and teamwork are essential for success. Employees who are able to ask for help when needed, delegate tasks effectively, and leverage the expertise of their colleagues are more likely to be seen as valuable team players and to contribute to the overall success of the organization.

The benefits of asking for help are not limited to external

achievements. On a personal level, seeking support can improve our mental and emotional well-being. When we are struggling with a problem or feeling overwhelmed, reaching out to others for help can reduce stress, anxiety, and feelings of isolation. It can also provide us with a fresh perspective, new ideas, and emotional support, all of which can contribute to a more positive and resilient outlook on life.

Moreover, asking for help can strengthen our relationships and deepen our connections with others. When we allow ourselves to be vulnerable and seek support from our loved ones, friends, and colleagues, we are demonstrating trust and opening the door for deeper connection. This can lead to stronger bonds, greater intimacy, and a more supportive and fulfilling social network.

Teaching children the importance of asking for help is a gift that will last a lifetime. It is a skill that will empower them to navigate challenges with resilience, build strong relationships, and access the resources and support they need to thrive. By modeling vulnerability, encouraging children to express their needs and concerns, and creating a safe and supportive environment where they feel comfortable asking for help, we can help them develop the confidence and resourcefulness necessary for success in all areas of life.

In addition to the immediate benefits, asking for help can have long-term implications for a child's personal and professional development. When children learn to seek support when needed, they are more likely to be seen as self-aware, resourceful, and collaborative. These qualities are highly valued in both personal and professional relationships and can open doors to opportunities in all areas of life.

Furthermore, asking for help can be a powerful tool for social change. When we recognize that we cannot solve all the world's problems alone, we are more likely to collaborate with others, pool our resources, and work together to create a more just and equitable society. Children who learn to ask for help and to offer support to others are more likely to become engaged citizens who actively participate in their communities and contribute to the greater good.

In conclusion, the act of asking for help is a courageous and empowering act. It is a recognition of our shared humanity, a willingness to be vulnerable, and a testament to our belief in the power of connection. For children, learning to ask for help is a journey of self-discovery, relationship building, and personal growth. By fostering a culture of support and encouragement, we can empower children to overcome challenges, achieve their goals, and live a more fulfilling and connected life. So, let us all embrace the power of asking for help and teach our children that it's okay to need support, for it is through our connections with others that we find our greatest strength and resilience.

ppp

It's okay to ask for help when you need it. We all need support sometimes, and reaching out for help is a sign of strength, not weakness. Remember, there are people who care about you and want to see you succeed.

TWENTY-FOUR

CELEBRATE YOUR SUCCESS! BE PROUD OF YOUR PROGRESS

In the grand tapestry of life, our journey is marked by a series of milestones, both big and small. These achievements, whether it's mastering a new skill, overcoming a challenge, or simply making progress towards our goals, deserve to be celebrated. The act of celebrating our successes is not merely an indulgence; it is a powerful practice that reinforces positive behaviors, boosts self-esteem, and fuels our motivation to continue striving for greatness. For young learners, embracing the joy of celebration is not just about reveling in accomplishments; it is a mindset that fosters a sense of self-efficacy, resilience, and a lifelong love of learning.

Imagine a child who has been diligently practicing their piano scales for weeks. At first, their fingers stumbled over the keys, and the melody was halting and uncertain. But with each practice session, their playing improved, their fingers gaining agility and confidence. Finally, they are able to perform the scales flawlessly, their music flowing effortlessly from their fingertips. In that moment, the child's face lights up with pride and joy, as they bask in the glow of their accomplishment. This celebration is not just a reward for their hard work; it is a validation of their efforts, a reinforcement of their growing skills, and a motivation to continue pursuing their musical passion.

The power of celebrating success lies in its ability to reinforce positive behaviors and create a sense of accomplishment. When we take the time to acknowledge and celebrate our achievements, we are signaling to ourselves that our efforts are worthwhile and that we are capable of achieving our goals. This positive feedback loop can be incredibly motivating, as it encourages us to continue striving for excellence and to set new and even more ambitious goals for ourselves.

For children, learning to celebrate their successes is a crucial step in developing a positive self-image and a healthy sense of self-worth. It is a skill that teaches them to recognize their own strengths and abilities, to appreciate their unique talents, and to take pride in their accomplishments. When children celebrate their successes, they are not only boosting their self-esteem but also reinforcing positive behaviors, such as perseverance, dedication, and hard work.

The impact of celebrating success extends beyond personal well-being. In academic settings, the act of celebrating student achievements can foster a positive and supportive learning environment. When teachers and parents acknowledge and celebrate the efforts and progress of their students, they are creating a culture of encouragement and appreciation that motivates students to continue striving for excellence. This can lead to improved academic performance, increased engagement, and a greater love of learning.

Furthermore, celebrating success is a valuable asset in the professional world. In the workplace, recognizing and celebrating employee achievements can boost morale, increase productivity, and foster a positive company culture. When employees feel valued and appreciated for their contributions, they are more likely to be engaged in their work, committed to the organization's goals, and motivated to go above and beyond their job descriptions.

The benefits of celebrating success are not limited to external achievements. On a personal level, celebrating our wins can bring us joy, satisfaction, and a sense of fulfillment. When we take the time to savor our accomplishments, we are allowing ourselves to fully experience the positive emotions associated with success, which can boost our mood, reduce stress, and enhance our overall well-being.

Moreover, celebrating success can strengthen our relationships and foster a sense of community. When we share our achievements with others and celebrate their successes, we are creating a positive feedback loop that reinforces positive behaviors, encourages mutual support, and builds stronger bonds.

Teaching children the importance of celebrating their successes is a gift that will last a lifetime. It is a skill that will empower them to recognize their own worth, appreciate their accomplishments, and cultivate a positive outlook on life. By modeling celebratory behaviors, providing children with opportunities to share their achievements, and encouraging them to celebrate the successes of others, we can help them develop a lifelong appreciation for the journey of growth and accomplishment.

In addition to the immediate benefits, celebrating success can have long-term implications for a child's personal and professional development. When children learn to recognize and appreciate their own achievements, they are more likely to be seen as confident, motivated, and successful individuals. These qualities are highly valued in both personal and professional relationships and can open doors to opportunities in all areas of life.

Furthermore, celebrating success can be a powerful tool for social change. When we celebrate the achievements of individuals from marginalized or underrepresented groups, we are challenging stereotypes, breaking down barriers, and creating a more inclusive and equitable society. Children who learn to celebrate diversity and recognize the achievements of others, regardless of their background or circumstances, are more likely to become compassionate and inclusive leaders who can make a positive impact on the world.

In conclusion, the act of celebrating success is more than just a fleeting moment of joy; it is a powerful practice that can transform our lives and the lives of those around us. For children, learning to celebrate their achievements is a journey of self-discovery, empowerment, and connection. By fostering a culture of celebration, we are not only teaching children to appreciate their own worth but also encouraging them to recognize and celebrate the unique talents and contributions of others. So, let us all embrace the power of celebration and use it to create a more joyful, supportive, and inclusive world for ourselves and for generations to come.

ᗞᗞᗞ

Take pride in your accomplishments, no matter how big or small. Celebrating your successes reinforces positive behaviors and motivates you to continue striving for greatness.

TWENTY-FIVE

YOUR VOICE MATTERS! SHARE YOUR THOUGHTS AND MAKE A DIFFERENCE

In the symphony of human existence, each individual possesses a unique voice, a melody that contributes to the richness and diversity of our collective experience. For young learners, understanding the power and significance of their voice is not just a matter of self-expression; it is a call to action, an invitation to participate in the grand conversation of life and to make a meaningful contribution to the world. It's a recognition that their thoughts, ideas, and perspectives matter, and that by sharing them with courage and conviction, they can inspire change, challenge norms, and create a more just and equitable society.

Imagine a child standing before a crowd, their heart pounding with a mixture of excitement and nervousness. They take a deep breath and begin to speak, their voice trembling at first but gradually gaining strength and clarity as they share their story, their dreams, and their vision for a better future. In that moment, the child is not just speaking; they are embodying the power of their voice, inspiring others with their passion and conviction.

The power of voice lies in its ability to connect, inspire, and transform. When we share our thoughts and ideas, we are not just communicating information; we are opening a window into our souls, inviting others to see the world through our eyes. This act of vulnerability can be incredibly powerful, as it creates a space for empathy, understanding, and connection.

For young learners, finding and using their voice is a journey of self-discovery, empowerment, and social engagement. It is a process that involves recognizing their own unique perspectives, developing the confidence to express their thoughts and feelings, and learning to use their voice to advocate for themselves and others. When children embrace the power of their voice, they are not only expressing themselves but also contributing to a more diverse and inclusive society.

The impact of using one's voice extends far beyond personal expression. In academic settings, the ability to articulate ideas clearly and persuasively is essential for success. Whether it's writing essays, giving presentations, or participating in class discussions, students who can use their voice effectively are more likely to be heard, respected, and valued.

Furthermore, using one's voice is a critical skill in the professional world. In today's fast-paced and competitive environment, individuals who can communicate their ideas with confidence and clarity are more likely to be seen as leaders and innovators. They are also more likely to be successful in job interviews, negotiations, and team collaborations.

The benefits of using one's voice are not limited to external achievements. On a personal level, expressing oneself authentically can lead to greater self-awareness, self-esteem, and overall well-being. When we speak our truth, we are honoring our own experiences and perspectives, which can lead to a stronger sense of self and a more fulfilling life.

Moreover, using one's voice can be a powerful tool for social change. Throughout history, individuals who have spoken out against injustice, advocated for equality, and shared their stories of struggle and triumph have inspired movements and transformed societies. Children who learn to use their voice to speak up for what they believe in can become powerful agents of change, creating a ripple effect that can positively impact their communities and the world.

Teaching children the importance of using their voice is a gift that will last a lifetime. It is a lesson that will empower them to express themselves authentically, advocate for their needs and beliefs, and make a meaningful contribution to society. By providing children with opportunities to share their thoughts and ideas, encouraging them to speak up for what they believe in, and celebrating their unique perspectives, we can help them develop the confidence and skills necessary to make their voices heard and their presence felt in the world.

In addition to the immediate benefits, using one's voice can have long-term implications for a child's personal and professional development. When children learn to communicate effectively and advocate for themselves, they are more likely to be seen as confident, assertive, and influential. These qualities are highly valued in both personal and professional relationships and can open doors to opportunities in all areas of life.

Furthermore, using one's voice can be a powerful tool for personal growth and self-discovery. When we express our thoughts and feelings, we are not only communicating with others but also gaining a deeper understanding of ourselves. This process of self-reflection can lead to greater self-awareness, personal growth, and a more authentic and fulfilling life.

In conclusion, the phrase "Your voice matters" is more than just an affirmation; it is a call to action, an invitation to embrace our unique perspectives and share them with the world. For young learners, discovering and using their voice is a journey of empowerment, self-discovery, and social engagement. By encouraging children to express themselves authentically, to advocate for what they believe in, and to use their voice to make a difference, we are nurturing the next generation of leaders, innovators, and changemakers. So, let us all embrace the power of our voices and use them to create a more just, equitable, and harmonious world for ourselves and for generations to come.

ᗐᗐᗐ

Your voice has the power to inspire change, so speak up and share your thoughts with the world. Your ideas matter, your opinions are valuable, and your voice can make a difference.

TWENTY-SIX
SUMMARY

Unleashing Your Inner Communicator: A Journey of Confidence and Connection

Effective communication is a fundamental cornerstone for thriving in our interconnected world. For young individuals, it's a journey of self-discovery, empowerment, and connection. By nurturing these skills early on, we equip them with the tools to navigate life's complexities, build lasting relationships, and make a positive impact on the world.

The Power of First Impressions:

The journey begins with a simple "Hello, World!" accompanied by a warm smile. This seemingly small gesture sets the stage for positive interactions, signaling openness, warmth, and a willingness to connect. A smile is a universal language that transcends cultural barriers and age differences, instantly putting others at ease and creating an atmosphere of approachability.

The Language of the Eyes:

Making eye contact is another powerful tool in the communicator's toolbox. It conveys attentiveness, respect, and a genuine interest in the other person. For young learners, mastering eye contact can boost their confidence and help them forge deeper connections with others. It's a nonverbal signal that says, "I see you, I hear you, and I value what you have to say."

The Art of Attentive Listening:

Listening is not merely about hearing words; it's about actively engaging with the speaker, absorbing their message, and responding with empathy and understanding. By paying attention, children not only gain knowledge but also develop critical thinking skills and build stronger relationships. It's a practice that fosters respect, promotes collaboration, and creates a safe space for open dialogue.

The Curiosity Catalyst:

Asking questions is a gateway to discovery and a testament to our innate thirst for knowledge. By encouraging children to ask "why" and "how," we ignite their curiosity and empower them to explore the world around them. It's a skill that cultivates critical thinking, problem-solving abilities, and a lifelong love of learning. Asking questions not only deepens our understanding but also strengthens our connections with others by demonstrating genuine interest in their thoughts and experiences.

The Ripple Effect of Kind Words:

Words possess immense power to uplift or tear down. Choosing kind words is a conscious act of compassion that creates a positive and nurturing environment for everyone. Compliments, words of encouragement, and expressions of gratitude can brighten someone's day, boost their confidence, and foster a sense of belonging. It's a reminder that even small acts of kindness can have a ripple effect, spreading joy and goodwill throughout our communities.

The Clarity of Expression:

Speaking clearly is essential for effective communication. By articulating our thoughts and feelings with precision, we ensure that our message is understood and appreciated by others. For children, mastering clear speech builds confidence and empowers them to express themselves authentically. It's a skill that opens doors to academic success, professional achievement, and personal fulfillment.

The Language of the Body:

Our bodies are constantly communicating, often revealing more than our words ever could. Posture, gestures, and facial expressions all contribute to the unspoken language of nonverbal communication. Understanding and interpreting these cues can help children navigate social situations with greater ease, build stronger relationships, and express themselves more effectively.

The Healing Power of Dialogue:

When conflicts arise, the instinct to avoid or suppress them can be tempting. However, talking it out offers a path to resolution, understanding, and growth. By encouraging children to express their feelings, listen to others with empathy, and work collaboratively to find solutions, we equip them with essential conflict resolution skills that will serve them well throughout their lives.

The Confidence of Posture:

Standing tall is not just about physical alignment; it's a reflection of our inner confidence and self-assurance. By encouraging children to stand tall, we are empowering them to embrace their individuality, own their space, and project an image of confidence that can inspire others.

Embracing Differences:

In a world of diverse opinions, learning to disagree respectfully is a crucial skill. By teaching children to value different perspectives, listen with an open mind, and express their own views in a constructive manner, we are fostering a culture of tolerance, empathy, and understanding.

The Joy of Celebration:

Celebrating our successes, no matter how big or small, is essential for reinforcing positive behaviors and maintaining motivation. By acknowledging and appreciating our achievements, we create a positive feedback loop that encourages us to continue striving for excellence. It's a reminder that the journey of growth is filled with milestones worth celebrating, and that each step forward is a testament to our resilience and determination.

The Authenticity Advantage:

In a world that often encourages conformity, being true to oneself is a radical act of self-love and empowerment. By embracing their unique personalities, interests, and passions, children can forge deeper connections with others, express themselves authentically, and live a more fulfilling life.

The Creative Spark of Imagination:

Imagination is the wellspring of creativity, innovation, and problem-solving. By encouraging children to use their imagination to tell stories, share ideas, and explore new possibilities, we are nurturing their creativity, expanding their horizons, and empowering them to shape the world around them.

The Persistence of Practice:

The path to mastery in any skill, including communication, is paved with practice. The more we engage in the art of conversation, the more natural and effortless it becomes. By providing children with opportunities to practice their communication skills in a safe and supportive environment, we can help them build confidence, refine their abilities, and develop a lifelong love of learning.

The Courage to Seek Help:

Asking for help is not a sign of weakness but a testament to our courage and self-awareness. By encouraging children to seek guidance and support when needed, we are teaching them to embrace vulnerability, build resilience, and tap into the collective wisdom of others.

In conclusion, the journey of effective communication is a lifelong adventure, filled with opportunities for growth, connection, and self-discovery. By nurturing these essential skills in our young learners, we are empowering them to become confident, empathetic, and articulate individuals who can make a positive impact on the world. So, let us all embrace the power of communication and use it to build bridges, foster understanding, and create a more connected and compassionate world.

ᗰᗰᗰ

Citation And References

This book represents the culmination of extensive research and meticulous analysis, incorporating a diverse range of sources, including numerous books, scholarly studies, and personal experiences. Additionally, I have scoured various websites to gather relevant information and data essential for the compilation of this work. I have taken every precaution to ensure the accuracy of the information presented and have diligently cited all sources to acknowledge their contributions.

Despite these efforts, the possibility of inadvertent errors remains. I deeply value the insights of my readers and appreciate any feedback that can help identify and rectify such inaccuracies. I encourage you to bring any discrepancies to my attention.

Your feedback is not only welcome but crucial, as it will aid in correcting current editions and enhancing the content of future ones. I am committed to maintaining the highest standards of accuracy and reliability in my work and thank you for your support and understanding.

Additionally, I firmly uphold the principle of freedom of speech and expression as guaranteed under Article 19(1)(a) of the Constitution of India, and I respect the diverse viewpoints and expressions of all readers.

ᐅᐅᐅ

Other Books Of The Author

1. Empowering Minds: A Journey into Women's Self-Discovery and Power
2. The Dynamics of Motivation: Catalyzing Thought into Action
3. Meditation and Mental Well Being: The Path to Inner Peace and Clarity
4. The Psychology of Child Education: Nurturing Future Generations
5. Ethical Enlightenment: A Modern Guide to Living with Integrity
6. Voices of Empowerment: Stories of Women Rising Against Odds
7. Social Psychology in Everyday Life: Understanding Human Connections
8. The Essence of Motivational Speaking: Inspiring Change in Others
9. Balancing Acts: Women, Work, and the Will to Lead
10. Guiding with Grace: Raising Children with Compassion and Awareness
11. The Power of Positive Aging: Embracing Life After Fifty
12. Building Resilient Communities: Social Work in Action
13. The Ethical Educator: Principles for Teaching and Learning
14. From Insight to Impact: Social Psychology for a Better World
15. The Ethics of Empathy: A Guide to Ethical Living
16. The Science of Empowering the Self: Navigating Life's Challenges with Psychological Wisdom
17. The Mindful Conscious Leader: Meditation Techniques for Modern Management
18. Pioneering Spirit: Women's Pathways to Leadership and Empowerment
19. Feeling to Healing: The Role of Emotional Intelligence in Child Development
20. Transformative Talks and Words of Inspiration: Insights into Motivational Oratory

21. Green Ethics: A Path to Sustainable Living
22. Spiritual Integrity: Navigating Life with Moral Compassion
23. Clean Living, Clean Society: The Ethics of Cleanliness
24. Patriotic Spirits: Building a Nation on Positive Attitudes
25. Innovative Integrity & Vibrant Visions: The Ethical and Entrepreneurial Spirit of Gujarat
26. Youthful Visions, Endless Possibilities: Inspiring Ethics and Motivation in Children
27. Living Your Legacy: How to Motivate Others by Living Your Values
28. Secret of Healing Conversations: Ethical Practices in Counselling and Therapy
29. Creative Kindness: Crafting a Life of Compassion and Creativity
30. The Power of Appreciation: How Gratitude Can Transform Your Relationships
31. Bhagavad-Gita: Messages
32. Science of Art: The New Frontier of Fashion Modernism
33. Vivekananda's Virtues: A Blueprint for Modern Living
34. Empower Her: Navigating the Path to Women's Entrepreneurship
35. The Boundless Classroom: Innovations in Global Education
36. The Language of Leadership: Communicating with Authenticity and Impact
37. The Warrior's Mantra: Deciphering the Hanuman Chalisa
38. Echoes of Empathy: Transformative Stories of Social Service
39. Artful Living: Cultivating Creativity in Your Daily Routine
40. Finding Your Why: Discovering Your Passions and Charting Your Course
41. The Role of Social Media in Shaping Self-Esteem and Interpersonal Relationships among Adolescents
42. Karma's Tapestry: Weaving a Life of Selfless Service
43. Altruistic Alchemy: Transforming Lives Through Giving
44. The Blueprint of Pro-Activeness and Productivity: Crafting Habits for Success
45. The Simplicity with Grounded Wisdom: Embracing Authenticity

in a Complex World

46. Secret of Solopreneur's Odyssey: Navigating the Path to Self-Employment
47. Exploring Tapestry of Peace: Global Perspectives on Harmony
48. The Art and Actions of Connection: Mastering Communication for Impact
49. She Governs and at the Helm: Strategies for Political Empowerment
50. Rising Above and Rising with Grace: A Woman's Roadmap to Career Mastery
51. The Effect of Networking & Connectedness: Building Strategic Alliances for Women
52. Beyond his Barriers: Women Thriving in Male-Dominated Fields
53. Secret of Inner Compass: Navigating Life with Intuition
54. Creative & Pro-Active Muses: A Celebration of Women in the Arts
55. Unburdened: The Art of Releasing the Past
56. Amplified Voices: Speeches of Women that Astonished the World
57. Secret of Manifesting Dreams: A Woman's Guide to Intentional Living
58. Ethics and Value Based Education: Reimagining Japan's School System
59. The Moral Compass Curriculum: A Holistic Approach
60. Tech with Heart: Integrating Ethics into Digital Learning
61. Honoring Virtue: Recognizing Ethical Excellence in Education
62. Raising Good Humans: A Guide to Character Development
63. The Spark Within: Nurturing Creativity in Children
64. The Teenager Whisperer: Navigating Adolescence with Grace
65. Igniting a Passion for Learning: Inspiring Lifelong Curiosity
66. The Habit Lab: Cultivating Positive Behaviors in Children
67. Seeds of Empathy: Fostering Compassion in Young Hearts
68. The Reading Revolution: Inspiring a Love of Books in Children
69. The Learning Brain: Unlocking the Secrets of Student Success
70. Teaching for All: Differentiated Instruction Strategies
71. The Time Alchemist: Mastering Time Management for Peak Performance

72. The Resilience Factor: Transforming Setbacks into Stepping Stones
73. The Healing Touch of Nature: An Introduction to Naturopathy
74. Echoes of the Past: Healing Through Past Life Regression
75. The Spiritual Healer's Handbook: Exploring Energy Medicine
76. Crystal Clarity: Unveiling the Power of Gemstones
77. The Dream Weaver's Guide: Decoding the Language of Dreams
78. Emotional Alchemy: Transforming Pain into Power
79. Sonic Serenity: Harnessing Sound for Stress Relief
80. The Entrepreneur's Playbook: Launching Your Business with Confidence
81. Productivity Unleashed: Time Management Strategies for Entrepreneurs
82. The Problem Solver's Toolkit: Creative Solutions for Business Challenges
83. The Future is Now: Emerging Trends in Business
84. The Curious Explorer: A Child's Guide to Scientific Discovery
85. Digital Pioneers: Empowering Kids in the Tech World
86. The Young Philosopher's Guide: Exploring Life's Big Questions
87. Finding Your Voice: Communication Skills for Confident Kids
88. Nature's Playground: A Child's Guide to Outdoor Adventure
89. Growing a Greener Tomorrow: A Guide to Tree Planting & Conservation
90. Driving with Purpose: Ethical Choices on the Road
91. The Healing Touch: Cultivating Compassion in Healthcare
92. Navigating the Digital Landscape: Ethics in the Age of Social Media
93. The Ethical Closet: A Guide to Sustainable Fashion
94. The Mindful Voyager: Sustainable Travel Practices
95. The Feminine Divine: Honoring the Goddesses of India
96. Sacred Sounds: Chanting Your Way to Inner Peace
97. The Yoga Path: Uniting with the Divine Within
98. Rites of Passage: Creating Meaningful Ceremonies
99. The Chakra System: A Map of Inner Transformation
100. Spiritual Sangha: Finding Community through Satsang and

Bhajan

101. Pilgrimage of the Soul: Spiritual Journeys in India

ᏜᏜᏜ

Contact

Dr. Minakshi Bansal
Social Activist
Ahmedabad, Gujarat, Bharat
minakshiindiag20@yahoo.com

❦❦❦

|| LOKAHA SAMASTHAHA SUKHINO BHAVANTU ||